# My Only One

HIMABINDU NIMMA



BlueRose ONE.com
Stories Matter
NewDelhi • London

**BLUEROSE PUBLISHERS**
India | U.K.



BlueRose ONE
Stories Matter
NewDelhi • London

For permissions requests or inquiries regarding this publication, please contact:

BLUEROSE PUBLISHERS
www.BlueRoseONE.com
info@bluerosepublishers.com
+91 8882 898 898
+4407342408967

ISBN: 978-93-5989-898-8

Cover design: Tahira
Typesetting: Tanya Raj Upadhyay

First Edition: May 2024

DEDICATED TO

I dedicate this book to Sunanda, my friend

to whom I never got the chance to tell

my unspoken words.

# About the Author

The author of this book is HimaBindu Nimma. Her hometown is Balijipeta, near Bobbili, Andhra Pradesh from where she did her engineering, and is currently located in Hyderabad. She lives with her brother, and grandparents in Hyderabad whereas her parents live in hometown. She did her graduation from Swamy Vivekananda Engineering College, and currently works in Amazon as Investigator Specialist, previously was employed in Accenture as Business Operations Associate. Friends show a great impact in her life, she loves to spend time, and hang out with all her dear ones, she loves to be in the world of fantasies as it is a world where no barriers, no limits are there, and she could do crazy stuffs without anyone stopping her.

# Foreword

## " सखा त्वमेव "

Finding a bond between two hearts that goes beyond simple blood ties or commercial transactions is uncommon. The story that takes place in the pages that follow is a testament to the raw bond of friendship, written by a remarkable person.

You will experience a range of emotions as you explore the depths of these stories, with every scene capturing the reality of life's journey. While every individual is inherently a friend to all, we will see here a friend who becomes an entire universe to my dear friend.

Even when her best friend faces unforeseen obstacles in life, HimaBindu's everlasting commitment and true affection is evident. This work of writing will always have a particular place in the hearts of those who have valued the priceless connection of friendship.

Seeing Bindu's path is encouraging because it shows how strong she is and how she has remained true to love and honesty even in the face of adversity. A friend like her is truly a buddy for all time. It's amazing to witness Bindu reach such great success.

**Jai ShriRam.**

Vivekanand Vemakoti

B.Tech, M.Tech, M.B.A.,M.A

Assistant Professor

# Preface

I would like to take a moment here. How many of you people remember your college days? When I asked you this question I reminisced mine. You would have remembered your gang or that person with whom you used to stick on, right! I too had such a beautiful gang, and that one person (Sunanda) who made my life worth living. Back then when I joined college, I just wanted those four years to finish in seconds but once I graduated, I wished to go back in college time, and to relive those moments. That's how much those days impact me.

Life was so good back then until one day, when destiny took its unexpected turn which resulted in publishing '*My Only One*'. She (Sunanda) introduced the new me to myself, making me publish this book. I never thought I would write a book for her, but a day came into my life when I turned all the trauma into words. The trauma was the distance. Did you ever miss your friend if he/she was not beside you? What if the next meet will gonna take a lifetime wait, will you wait? If it's a real time you obviously have to wait, and wait till the circumstances doesn't allow you. This book shows the journey of growing friendship, and the waiting time that we both went through to meet each other, did I meet her again after distance or am I still waiting for her to come back to me? To know the answer, you have to read this beautiful journey of friendship between me, and my only one.

It's been almost four years since I have written this book but got an opportunity to publish it now. I was a normal girl until she came into my life, and had it not been for her I would have never thought of publishing something this way.

# Acknowledgement

It was a very challenging journey as whenever I thought that it's getting done, there came unexpected twists but finally thanks to Krishnayya, I believe in your path that you show me when things are apart and for helping me manifest my dream come true.

I would like to thank the publishing house BlueRose Publisher's, and to its entire publishing team who helped me in fulfilling my dream.

My special thanks to Vivek sir who had been a great support to me from the beginning when I told him about this book. Thank you, sir for believing in me when I felt I couldn't make it come to this far. Without you this path would definitely had been a bumpy one. I'll be forever grateful to you.

To Surya, thank you for giving your precious time to this book, and giving the positive feedback which actually boosted my confidence, and made me take a step to publish it.

Sunanda, though it's written for you, it's again a gift to myself. Trying to break all the odds as much as I can and with this I hope our families and friends be delighted.

# 1

Surprisingly, the day had come. I woke up from my dreams, and started to daydream that, within four years, I will be an engineer. On that day, I only knew that I was going to college for my studies, and to have some fun, as every student do in their life. However, I never knew that these four years would change my life, and I would get an experience that one experiences only once in a lifetime.

I got ready for my first day at college with a bit of excitement, or I should say with no excitement at all. Everyone says that college is a place where we will have so much fun, make friends, find love, experience seniors ragging, etc., just like they show in movies. However, nothing made me feel fascinated because I wanted to study in Hyderabad with one of my childhood friends, and to my destiny, I returned to my hometown. As of now, I feel that step has changed my life.

I remember what I wore that day, just like most of the people remember when they are going through a different phase of life. I think one tends to focus on every single detail at certain times, like the happiest, and the saddest days. I wore a white top with black bandini-style dots all over it, and black border emphasizing around the neck, along with black leggings, and a basic black dupatta. Those were the days when girls were supposed to wear dupattas mandatorily to college, or else we would be "attacked" by the seniors, as per some information I got from other people. Anyway, I was living in my hometown at that time with certain strict rules, so I appeared a bit more traditional.

I kissed my mom, and bid her goodbye. She looked at me till I was visible to her. She has kept on doing this since my school days, and it was her habit to look at me until I vanished from the street. I feel that in her heart, she might be thinking that my girl has grown up, and now she is in college. May she be blessed with a good future, and may Durga devi support, and strengthen her every time. The love of a mom is so precious; she doesn't need to say "I love you"; it is expressed in everything she does.

I walked, smiling, and thinking about her abundance of love for me. Then I spotted something. There was a yellow-painted bus with "Swamy Vivekananda Engineering College" written on it; in short, SVEB (college code). Yeah, so that was the bus that I'm supposed to take to reach my destination, and of course, it continues for a long, boring four years. I stepped on the bus, and it started moving. The college is approximately 45 minutes from my home. In India, we have a habit of saying distance in the form of time, not in kilometers, and somehow, it is a beneficial thing as we can estimate how much time it is going to take.

I saw a few students getting on the bus—some seniors, and some freshers like me. People who knew each other were cracking jokes; some were excited, and some were nervous. I started to think about my life, my future, when, and where this journey ends, up to how long I'm going to travel through this bus, and some other stuff that was going on.

Soon there was a brake on the bus as well as on my thoughts as our college arrived; we had actually reached inside. I got down from the bus, and all the freshers were asked to sit in the auditorium, so we followed. It was a large hall filled with many chairs in six columns that extended to the end of the hall. The chairs, which were made of wood, were attached with a pad to take notes. I thought to myself that, in a rural place, having a college with good infrastructure was impressive. I was sitting in the middle row's second column while waiting for the principle to come.

Suddenly, I heard someone giggling too loudly, and saw a girl in the first column-second chair who was not able to sit quietly. She was so excited, feeling like she was the only girl who was happy in this whole world. She was talking to another girl, and couldn't resist sitting in her place, so she turned almost to her friend. I laughed in my mind, thinking how crazy she was. The latter one was sitting in the first column-first chair, and this girl was quite the opposite. She looked so cute, and so silent, though I couldn't see her completely, she appeared very calm. I saw some more people talking to each other. I felt like I was the alien in the whole room. Then the principal arrived, and distracted everyone from their businesses. He gave a speech, and welcomed us to the college, which was almost the top college of that area. He asked us to see the college premise, and advised us to interact with each other rather than being silent. When we all went out to see the college premise I saw that many people had come with their parents.

We saw the entire college. The college is so spacious with a giant gate at the entrance which is black-coated, and is supported by two giant walls on which "college name" was written with blue paint as a background, and white painted letters. Some security guards were making note of each entry, and exit. Ahead, there is a two-way road that was not concreted as of then, with trees in two columns welcoming everyone with greenery. There was a lot of space to park all the buses side by side, with some numbers on each front glass to identify the local area buses. A very large area in which the center of the college was located. The ground is filled with grass, making it look peaceful. Gardeners were cleaning the ground, and cutting the extra grown grass to make it appear pleasant enough. Some students were roaming in the ground in pink, and cement color combination dresses, which are college uniforms with a dark blue tag ID card. Yes, we have a uniform to wear for the entire four years, which contradicts many other colleges. The good thing is there won't be any greater or lesser feeling; everyone looks equal, just like in our schools.

The college is a three-story building, with some blocks separating each branch, and labs, a comfortable hangout place canteen, which is far from the entry view, and is the last block. The college faces a main road; heading that way, there are farms, and behind the college there are many trees. A local sports building side to the college, and big trees adjacent to the two sides of the college made it look good enough. We could see a beautiful channel flowing with clean water into the farms at a distance outside the college premises. Having a good view, I felt a bit pleasant in that place. Though I'm not interested in studying there, some reasons made me accept the situation, and I followed my destiny. I completed my admission, and other formalities, and chose the ECE (Electronics, and Communication Engineering) stream. Just as everyone says, by choosing ECE, you can go through either software or hardware. I was quite unaware of the purpose of choosing that stream, as that's a different field from the one I was in, irrespective of my planning. I thought for a while about my future after choosing this career path, and with no further queries to myself, I completed my admission, and left the place. That's how the first day of college ended, adding B.Tech day-one memories.

# 2

Days were passing by at a slow pace, and I felt it keenly because I was alone in the college. There were new faces, unfamiliar people, and no friends. I found myself alone, as all my childhood friends were studying elsewhere, dispersing due to our varied educational paths. Life took an unexpected turn, and I realized that the people you expect to be with may not always be part of your journey. As I commuted on the college bus, I pondered my family, and friends, realizing that my life revolves around them.

During my childhood, we lived in Hyderabad, a place that held a special place for me. It was where I was born, attended my first school, made my first friends, and experienced the joys of a small, close-knit family. Back then, my world was like an aquarium, and Hyderabad seemed like the entire universe. I was content, and carefree, and I believed I was the happiest girl on the planet.

Then came the day when I had to leave that small world behind. We shifted to our hometown, far away from Hyderabad. I was 12 years old when my mom, leaving her maternal family, moved us to my dad's paternal home. The emotional connections I had formed in Hyderabad became more profound, and I started to understand the impact of leaving one's familiar surroundings.

The departure day remains vivid in my memory. Sobbing uncontrollably as we boarded the train, I felt a pain I had never experienced before. Leaving behind my maternal grandparents, and my uncles with whom I shared a strong bond, was emotionally challenging. We reached our hometown in Vizianagaram district, Andhra Pradesh, known for Sri Krishnadevaraya Samsthanam, and its historical significance in battles, and powerful personalities who set some standards across the country.

Adjusting to the new world, school, and making new friends took time. However, the greenery, and aesthetic beauty of the farms in our hometown appealed to me. My parents enrolled my brother, and me in a local government school that was reputed for its quality education. Initially hesitant about the decision, I later appreciated the choice my parents made for us.

The school had a nostalgic touch, with a giant tree at the entrance, and a building surrounded by mango trees, where my dad had studied during his childhood. Despite not being in use, the block held sentimental value for me. The school, set in the countryside, featured newly constructed buildings surrounding a vast field covered in grass. The environment was pristine, and free from pollution, a stark contrast to city life.

The countryside experience included seeing bullock carts as transportation, a sight that excited me as I had only read about them in books. Experiencing things firsthand, which were previously confined to textbooks, brought a unique enthusiasm. It reinforced the idea that joy often lies in appreciating the smallest things. As the bus reached my stop, the school itself (we boarded the college bus in front of the school), my thoughts took a break too.

# 3

In the beginning of my college days, I used to sit on the first bench. Then suddenly one day, a batch occupied the first row. I noticed that, and with no regrets, I sat in the second row. While taking my books out of my bag, I heard the same voice I heard at day one. The same girl was sitting in the first row, in third place. She turned back, and looked at me with a great smile on her face. I greeted her with a smile. I still remember her first conversation with me. She said, “Hi! I’m Sunanda.” I replied, "Hi, I'm Bindu.” She then asked me where I’m from, and started talking about herself, her area, her friends, and those who were sitting beside her. The other silent girl I saw on day one just smiled, and said hi, while Sunanda introduced her as Sravani. She introduced all her other bench mates. She couldn't be silent for a single second, I thought to myself, and I engaged in my work.

I used to be with only one girl, and talk to her. Meanwhile, this lively girl found her group. I wondered how she could have so many friends in such a short time. But that's a good thing, right?

Only a few people can get so close easily. On that evening, when I was going back from college, she called me, and offered me chocolate. I kindly said no. Soon, I saw her wide smile getting narrower. I got into the bus, and sat beside a girl; she was one of the students whom I saw at day one along with a group of her friends while traveling in the bus. I forgot my wallet at first day, and she was the one who gave me money to reach back home. She said her name was Mounika, and we had a general conversation on the bus. Going to college, and returning home became my daily routine.

Our bus used to go in between the farms, offering a keen vision of nature. I fell in love with its beauty. The farmers were working on the fields while the sun emerged slowly, feeling shy as it had been hidden the night before. The ponds reflected the Sky on the Earth, and birds dipped into the water for early morning showers. The way birds flew over the green farms, experiencing freedom, and trying to reach as high as possible, fascinated me. The big trees provided nests for the birds, and they sang, welcoming a good day. I again went back to my world by looking outside the window, and engaging myself.

I had a group of four girls in school when we settled in our hometown, and I liked them as they mingled within no time. From school to junior college, I was with them, and had many more memories. Later, I was the only girl coming, and going back home alone. I really missed them a lot. Maybe that's a reason I wanted to be alone during the initial days of college. But I tell you, B.Tech or any other degree, this graduation period won't let anyone be lost, and so happened in my life.

It could be almost a month or two, probably August, a day before friendship day. We came to college, attended lectures, and in the evening, while going home, Sunanda came to me, and gave me chocolate again. This time I accepted not because I wanted to, but just not to let the curve of a smile on her face get shrunk in the gloom. She felt even brighter this time; I could see the shine on her face. I smiled, saying thank you. She asked me what's special for next day, as it was Friendship day. I said nothing much. All my friends were in different places. I'm alone. She said with a bit of anger, "So I'm not your friend, right?" That word put some weight on my heart. I don't know why, but even to this day, I remember her words with that expression, looking straight into my eyes.

All my childhood friends called me on Friendship day. We wished each other well, and had a conference call for more than an hour. My mom is always a great supporter of me. Every secret of mine was first known to her. Having a mom who always supports, and encourages you is always a blessing. So, I was alone in college itself in the beginning, but when I reached home, the way she treated me made me feel more comfortable, and I had no other thoughts.

Within a few days, Sunanda started talking to me more, sitting beside me, having lunch together, and even making me a person in her new batch, where we totally became seven members with four girls, and three boys. I slowly started being comfortable with them, having fun, and was gradually coming out of loneliness. Let me tell you how the batch was: Sunanda, Sravani, Mounika, Bindu, and boys Nani, Tony, and Prasanna. Out of all, Sunanda is a very hyperactive girl, and Sravs is cute, and calm. I liked her innocence. Mouni is silent when she knows no one, but when she mingles, she can't shut her mouth. Nani is a loyal boy towards friendship. Tony, and Prasanna looked a bit similar in physical appearance, and behavior as well. At first, I thought both were brothers. I became a part of the group within no time.

We used to talk among each other during classes, we used to eat some snacks, and one day, all of a sudden, we decided to occupy the last bench.

We four girls sat on the last bench of the girl's column, and those three guys in theirs. At times, we were asked to stand up because of the noises we made during the lectures. Every student knows what the last bench is meant to them. It's a zone of comfort, attitude, mesmerizing moments, and what not? It's everything.

Sunanda always wanted to be by my side. She wanted to talk to me more than others, and started sharing her secrets that she had never shared before with anyone in college. After getting to know her a bit, I then thought about what made her a cheerful girl with a smile that was always on her face. She is the one who tried to make our friendship grow stronger. I too started getting to know her, but my mind used to alert me because of my previous loneliness, and that never won.

I may not recall all my B.Tech memories, as those moments, and those smiles are more than this book goes on. But I can manage with some precious, and also awful moments to add here. Once in our physics lab, Sunanda gave me her wristwatch, and told me, "From today onwards, we are going to exchange our watches." I said, "Okay", and later we exchanged them completely, she used to have my watch every time, and so do I. In English communication class, we were in the auditorium, and our lecturer asked two students to come, and read the dialogues, and have a conversation, which is a part of the communication class. Both she, and I looked at each other, and with a small gesture, we went, and delivered our dialogues as if we were acting in a movie rehearsal. She took slow steps, coming into my heart.

B.Tech is not only about enjoyment; it's also about studies. Actually, this is what we came for. As expected, we had our mid-exams soon. I have to mention that Sravani is a bookworm. All of us thought that we could study a day before exams, but Sravani started studying from day one. We got to know about this later; the latter one is Mouni. Being in the smart tech world in this generation, we used our phones to capture most of the notes, they sat in our album waiting for us, and we touched them a day before the exam. I wonder what kind of expressions they make!

Everyone was studying. The topper's batch was doing revision in which Sravs, and Mouni were there. Our boys opened their books after coming to college; some studied at night before the exam, just like me, and Sunanda. In the morning hours, exams were conducted, and the afternoon was for the preparation of the next day's paper. After morning exams, some started studying, some were listening to songs, and our batch of people were sitting at the usual place. Sunanda said, "Let's watch a short film." I asked, "Now?" with an exclamation mark on my face. She replied, "Yes, I just feel so", and winked. Knowing her craziness, we started watching a short film she suggested. She's a bit of a crazy girl, as I said from the beginning; she lived in an imaginary world just like me with her kind of fantasies. Pausing the video, she said, "Why can't we direct a short film of our own?" All of us gave her a surprising look. From that day on, she started coming up with ideas. "Let's do this sort of plot; I even thought of the scenarios, and the stuff." We all laughed out loud, and she gave her sarcastic look. We haven't directed, but with her imagination, we performed a stage skit the next year in college on Fresher's day.

# 4

One fine day, it was Sravani's birthday. Both Sunanda, and Sravani lived in the same town, Parvathipuram. Sunanda had invited me to her home many times, but I used to say, "Let's see in the future." We used to get ten days of Dussehra holidays every year in college, and it is my favorite festival. I used to do pooja at home for all ten days, worshipping Durga devi, as per my mom's suggestion. After completing pooja, and all things, I got ready to go to their place because that was the time she ordered, "At least with this reason, you just come home." So, I started from Balijipeta, where I used to live. It's approximately a one, and a half-hour to two hours journey to reach there, and I must catch two buses, one from Balijipeta to Bobbili (a very royal historical place), and one from Bobbili to Parvathipuram. Soon, I stepped into Bobbili, all three boys came, we all caught another bus, and reached our destination. The only girl missing is Mouni, since she was busy at home that day.

We all reached Parvathipuram complex. Sunanda was waiting for us there, and took all of us to her home. No one was there in the home; her mom, and dad were on duty. Her little, cute sister was also out. After a while, we all settled down in the house, cracking jokes at each other. Then I saw a cute, and very active girl entering the home. She's Srija, Sunanda's only little sister. As soon as she saw me, she hugged me so tightly with so much emotion, and love. From that day onwards, I felt like she is not only her sister but also mine.

That hug itself was enough to form a bond. I don't know how this elder, and younger sister got so connected with me in the first meeting itself, but it's so pure, and sacred. Later, her dad came with soft drinks, and snacks for us. I greeted her dad. Meanwhile, Sravs was calling us continuously, and yelling at all of us, "Did you guys come to wish me or you simply want to stay there?" in her cute voice with a bit of anger. We then started moving towards Sravs home; on the way, we bought a cake, and reached her home. All of us greeted her parents, and we all went into a room, and started enjoying like anything. We also talked to Mouni on phone just to let her know what she missed on that day. It's fun to tease our friend who is missing on one of the main occasions, right?

By afternoon, aunty prepared very delicious food. After that, we again had more fun talking about some more naughty, and silly things that every batch does. In the evening, we made her cut the cake, and once again, we all wished her, and left the place after some time. I hadn't seen Sunanda's mom, so again, we all went there just to see her. Her mother is just like mine; she is so caring, and so sweet. She too hugged me as soon as we met, and then she said, "You know, Sunanda always talks about you, Bindu. She treats you as her bestie." I felt so happy listening that she not only talks to me in college but also talks about me at her home, and that's a reason aunty always wanted to see me when she talked to me over the phone. While leaving, we all waved back to her parents, I gave a chocolate to my new little sister, I touched aunty's feet to take her blessings, and we left the place. That was one of the memorable days we had, as it was our first-time going to their place, and day by day we all were getting closer, especially my bond with Sunanda, is getting stronger.

Sunanda was feeling so dull one time. She came to college, and sat beside me. She was not having direct eye contact with me. I thought something was wrong. I asked her, she didn't utter a word. Without any question, she used to say everything, and used to speak throughout the day, but that day she was unable to speak a word. I kept on asking her, but she didn't answer me. I haven't ever seen her like that, and I didn't feel good as she was in bad mood. I too had my mood change, and then I understood that something hurt her the most or some past might have striked in her head. After seeing her that way, gathering all the confidence, I walked beside her, and told her just one thing: "You have to tell your pain at least to a single person in this world, might be your mom, your friend, or someone whom you trust, because if you keep it within yourself, it definitely won't work. Believe me, if you can't share with me, tell someone else because I can't see you like this, and I want my girl to be happy all the time." I don't know how much it impacted her. She told me all her miseries, the way she was since childhood, the problems that she faced until then, and most importantly, her bestie in childhood, whom she lost forever, and was not able to see one last time. Just to forget all those sufferings, she was more active, and energetic in college. Then that day, I got to know the pain behind her beautiful smile. She said,

"I don't know why I can see my bestie in you; that's a reason I wanted to make you a friend of mine." I realized why she got dull on the day before friendship day because of my words. I scolded myself for that arrogant behavior. Her name was Nimisha. She kept on talking about her, the bond that she had with that girl, and every small detail regarding her. I consoled her with my words. She felt much better, and I was happy that she came out of that mood. We simply try to judge a person by looking at them from afar, just as I did on the first day of college, and then when we get to know what the person is, we start understanding everything, and think from that new perspective.

From that day on, I too had that invisible thread binding more, and more between us, making our friendship stronger. I felt like she is such a sweetheart with such a good soul. Days were passing quickly, and so our bond is getting stronger. At times, our batch used to be a bit jealous about that; we enjoyed that too. There were festivals coming, and going, and when it was a holiday, we used to have conversations on calls, and speak about the whole day routine we had. For holidays, my childhood besties used to come home, and we all had a small get-together. I told them about my new friends. They all felt happy because I'm happy in the new place.

For every birthday in the batch, we used to cut cake, have fun, and buy some gifts. We were reaching the end of the year. It was just a span of 5–6 months, but we all got sunk in a sea called friendship that we were floating on with a unique feeling, and I tell you, that's the age most of the students feel so because that friendship makes you much stronger, and much better. It makes one go crazy, and we were living in our teens completely.

In B.Tech, we have roll numbers that are unique for everyone. All the students used to laugh at Sunanda's roll number every time when she was called by that number just because it's more unique than others, which ended with 420, and this somehow made her known in the entire college. Our lecturers, and we people called her with that number at times, and made her feel annoyed; she couldn't say no at least to the lecturers but rather had to bear that for the long four years.

# 5

## THE FIRST FIGHT

It became a daily routine to go to college, and come back home, doing assignments, records, etc. All of a sudden, one day, we were having fun, and in the midst of it, there was a fight between me, and Sunanda. I got so angry with her that I uttered, "I hate you." She laughed at me, and responded, "But I always love you", and left the place. Later, she was so dull because of my hurtful words. Mostly, I don't get angry easily, but if I do, I become such a hyper girl that I lose control of my tongue.

We stopped talking to each other for two days, and all our friends tried to make everything normal, but we didn't. It was so hard not to talk to her because we used to communicate even during classes but then, we had our lunch on separate benches just to show anger towards each other. We didn't like to mingle in our batch, choosing to be apart from each other. It was hard, but still, we remained distant. I approached her after I cooled down, and asked her, "Can we talk for a while?" to which she simply nodded. We both sat on a bench opposite each other, and she started crying. I wiped her tears, and hugged her. The very next day, she wrote a letter to me about how distant we were during those two days. I read that, and asked what's all that, she smiled, and said, "Those are my feelings I thought to tell you for the last two days, but we were not talking na, so I wrote a letter." We laughed, and everyone was happy that we both finally patched up. It's not only in love; breakups, and patch-ups happen, but also happens in friendship. The rest of the batch had a doubt about what caused our argument, and subsequent silence. We looked at each other, laughed, and never said a word to any of them. It's not a secret but we felt like keeping it as one of our hidden secrets.

From then on, every time we had a fight or couldn't speak to each other face-to-face, we used to write a letter. It worked so effectively, bringing a tremendous change in both of us, and helping us accept each other's flaws, and get to know each other's best by simply putting a pen on white paper. That's the best way to speak without speaking I found in Nandu. I call her Nandu, and she calls me Hima, only in specific situations like when we feel overwhelmed or excited. Throughout our entire B.Tech lives, we called each other by those names hardly a few times, but it's cool to do so. After the fight, she changed her name in my mobile, and she already has my name as Hima with two little hearts, but we just call each other normally as Sunanda, and Bindu. A small fight ended up with such a sweet memory.

A few days later, we all thought that we should go out, everyone was suggesting options like a restaurant or shopping. Bobbili is a place known for its kingdom, so why not we visit the fort? Everyone was sharing their views, but I suggested not all of them, the place is very well known for its Venugopal Swamy temple, a temple of Lord Shree Krishna, and its view would be so nice, especially the idol in the temple attracts one with all their heart, mind, and soul. So, we decided to go there. I don't know how fortunate we were, by the time we reached there, it was afternoon, and the temple was closed. I felt so disappointed because not visiting a temple for the first time all together made it feel like a bad sign. They all cheered me up, and Sunanda looked around, saw another temple that was open exactly opposite to that. She took me there, and said, "God is everywhere, right? All gods are the same, so just offer your prayers here. Let's come back next time. Don't be so childish." I cheered up, and we all visited the temple. While going back, we saw a road being constructed, we all placed our feet there, feeling as if we were the rulers of that place because we made our footprints at that spot. It was a good day for all of us, and we went back home happily.

# 6

It's the beginning of the new year. We all were very excited to welcome the new year. My childhood friends came to our hometown. The night before, we all gathered, bought a cake, enjoyed that evening, and had lots of fun. We also drew rangoli near our home. Most of the girls love welcoming the new year by adding beautiful colors to the floor. Then the countdown began. Soon it was the next year, 2016. That year was such a memorable year in all our lives because that was the first new year after we met. Sunanda dropped me a message with new year greetings, and I too did the same. She told me she decorated the entire home, and also put rangoli on the floor. Meanwhile, my friends called me, we cut the cake, later we talked about how our lives were going on, cracking jokes in between. Later in the night, we slept; no one knew when we fell asleep. The next morning, after going home, I hugged my mom, and dad, we greeted each other for one more beautiful year ahead.

I dialed almost all the numbers in my contact list, and greeted every family member, and friend. I say it was mostly a good year, but also a bit not. As usual, we had our college, and then soon we were having Sankranti holidays. In India, people love these festivals, especially Sankranti. This is the season when farmers receive their first paddy, and do pooja, wishing for a beautiful year ahead not only for them but also for all the people they pray for selflessly. After the festival, we all used to bring our festive snacks daily to college until we empty the jars, and eat them so pleasantly whenever we were hungry, not hungry, bored, excited, whatever we kept on eating until we felt normal or tired of eating.

It's February, our midterms were on again, and in the middle of exams I had my birthday. I usually don't have a habit of celebrating my birthday. When I was a child, I remember I used to cut cake. After I grew up, I never felt like celebrating, but this time it was done because of Sunanda. She along with our group bought a dress for me, a pair of earrings, a bracelet, a letter for me, and all the things were packed as tiny packs of gifts. But that day was not so good for me as I was a bit upset because I, and Mouni had an argument a day before, so I was not interested in staying at college. I gave them a party, and later left for home. Sunanda pleased me a lot to stay back, I said, "I'm not in a good mood; moreover, it can ruin my day more if I stay here", and left the place. Later in the evening, she said, "I thought of giving you one of the best birthdays, but you totally spoiled it", and asked me whether I was feeling better. I replied that I was alright, and that's how the day ended. Talking to her made me feel light-hearted. There is some magic when we talk to that one particular person alone; all the worries disappear, and those memories make us remember them for a longer time.

We were having our midterms, one day Sravs was feeling so low that her health was not at all good, so we four girls skipped the exam that day as we already scored well in the 1st midterm. There were two midterms per semester, and we were supposed to write both of them but in certain cases we get permission if the first term had a good score. After getting permission from our lecturer, we took her to the auditorium. We were the only four girls in that big auditorium sitting on dais. Sravs was sleeping on my lap, and we started chitchatting. We didn't even remember that Sravs was in pain as soon as we all started sharing our past moments, good, and bad that touched the remaining three girls.

When we were listening to each other that day, at one point we realized that the bond among all of us girls got strengthened some more because of the time or situation, we didn't know, but we then thought that we could share our happiest or saddest moments with each other. Even Sravs kept her pain aside, and started listening to all that with half-closed eyes. After involving ourselves in an emotional state, we then cheered ourselves up by cracking jokes on the patient. This girl always used to tell a different pain story for every new day; one day she used to say I'm getting a headache, the other day hand pain, and leg pain, she even used to explain that in her childish manner, which ultimately turned into comedy. But she's such a cute, and innocent girl that we had in our batch. That's how pain also added to one of the memorable days in our diaries.

I used to have the habit of keeping a diary. Later, I found out that Sunanda also started writing a diary when I saw it in her bag one day. When I asked her, she replied, “Yes, I started writing a diary just after joining B.Tech.” It was such a coincidence that we felt, and that was the only similarity we had. For the rest of the things, I used to say something, and she said another. We never had an idea matching between us, that was always the thing for which we had funny or serious fights, and arguments.

She really didn't know where to hide her diary, so she used to carry it every day to college. One day, she herself came to me after completing her first diary, and asked, "Can you keep this with you? Because I don't have a place to keep it safe." I said, "I'll read it for sure." She smiled, and said, "Your wish." I carried that along with me, the whole night I read that, and I don't know when I slept. That was the first time I was reading someone's personal life in letters through a book. Those words can convey her pain, her happiness, and her beloved things. At the end of that diary, I found myself with wet eyes, and I realized I was crying; I don't know from when. It touched my heart that much. Her handwriting has the pain, and happiness, the ups, and downs, and the grief. Everything is clearly visible for me that I wasn't reading, but I could see her through those pages.

The next day I went to college, gave her a hug, and said, "Everything is going to be okay for your grief, and for your happiness, I assure your happiness gets multiplied." I understood how much she trusts me, and after reading that diary, I found many similarities between my diary, and hers. The main thing is the trust we both have in our friends. I read her diary, but I never made her read mine; had she read that, she would have felt the same. I used to maintain her diary as carefully as mine. In a page, I read that the first impression of her when she saw me was, "How tall this girl is! It seems she won't talk to anyone, and never mingle with many people. Later, she became the most important person in my life. I don't know how, but she is." I could see the special place in her heart for me in her writing.

# 7

Days started passing too quickly. We didn't even recognize that we were at the end of the first year of B.Tech days. Soon we were near to our semester. We were a bit nervous because it was our final exams, and we had to give our best in that. We used to maintain a timetable when we were at the edge, and we all discussed together which made the learning process easy for us to remember every concept. It was April. Why I'm mentioning this is because we were getting closer to Nandu's birthday. I even had a countdown for every day, less than a month, more 15 days, more 10 days, less than a week, and yes, it was April 18. I chuckled within myself with some twinkle in my eyes. So, if you ask me how do you know the twinkle in your eyes? There is no need for another person to see the twinkle in your eyes, when you have a special place for a person in your heart, that twinkle can be seen through your heart, it says how happy you are with that person. Sunanda never used to celebrate her birthdays so I thought of celebrating but same as mine she was not at all happy that day because of some family issues, and she said please don't make any plans. When I asked her, she told me the issue, I understood her, and felt not to celebrate because it would rather hurt her the most if I make any further arrangements. That night I talked to her, and gave some support to lighten her heart so that she could sleep soon because at that particular time she needed someone's love. Talking about birthday wishes, we never wished each other on birthdays at 12 o'clock. By that time, we just pray for each other's happiness, and long life. We only greeted each other with birthday wishes after a lot of anticipation, and thus made our days special. The next day she was not feeling well, I could see pain in her eyes. I went to her, and she leaned on my shoulder, unable to control herself, she cried out loudly. I soothed her, she was a bit better, and I succeeded in making her come out of that mood. Every time she leans her head on my shoulder, she couldn't escape from her pain, she just vents it out, and then feels consoled. After taking her sweet time, she used to say "There's some magic in your shoulder Hima, I can't be in a bad mood further, I feel so comfortable." I felt so happy listening to those words, at least I was able to make her feel happy without any questions. The thing is in some particular situations knowing the problem is not important, the way to get rid of the problem completely is to be focused on, you may think without knowing the entire problem how can I get rid of that, it happened in our situation though I don't know what happened completely, and of course the other person's love for us is equally important. She was back with her craziness from the next moment.

The other day after the exam we had our lunch talking to each other about the exam paper. Sunanda suddenly felt an urge to see my mom. She told me, "We are going to your home, now." I said astonishingly, "Now! How can we go, and come back again; can we plan on a weekend?" She declined my words by taking her wallet from the bag, held my hand, and winked which means let's go in her language, and she was so excited that we went home, it took the usual 45 minutes to travel. We had a cool conversation in the auto about our families, past days, and funny stuff. On the way, I showed her my inter college, my school. Then, we reached home.

Seeing my mom, she grabbed her hand, and hugged her as if she knew my mom from many years. Without any doubt my mom said it was Sunanda because that's how much I told her about my girl. She chit chatted with my mom, and asked many questions about me, complained about me, and my mom told her all my childhood memories that she remembered. We stayed there for about an hour, before leaving, my mom presented her some traditional things that mostly Hindus do. She touched my mom's foot for blessings just like I did when I was in her home, and suddenly they both became emotional. I didn't understand what made them so close in less than an hour that they both had wet eyes. It was a heart touching moment, and a memory that engraved in my heart. I smiled within, and we both left the place. She said, "I feel your mom is just like my mom." I remembered that I too had the same feeling when I saw her mom. On the way back, she felt like eating something, and asked me to buy some snacks. I wanted to give her a treat for some reason, maybe it's because she made my mom happy or maybe she herself is so happy after a time being. I told her, "I will, but not something. I'll buy some of your favourites." She exclaimed, "Oh really! Let's see" by letting the kid in her heart awake. I took her to a nearby shop, and bought Amla (gooseberries) which is her favourite. I could see her mouth-watering by the time she saw them. She became a total kid, and was excited. She was eating them while we went to another shop, and I bought some chocolates. She kept them in her wallet. Later, we went to a bakery, and bought all the items that she liked to eat, also we made a parcel for the rest of the gang. We were waiting for an auto. There was no place in the auto, so we had to sit back because we were running out of time, and again, she was supposed to catch the college bus to reach her home. We sat there, and were eating, talking, laughing for nothing but something mischievous, that time we were heart filled with happiness. She made me take a video for those moments, so I started recording. She was telling how happy she was, and teased me at times. We cracked jokes on each other, and that's how the video was with such childish behavior. Soon after reaching college, she narrated everything to our friends, showed that video, and gave some snacks to them. They were a bit jealous for not joining us but we asked them to come. At that time none were interested, later they felt a bit low by thinking how much they missed. We cheered them up with snacks. It might look like a small moment but it had one of the most wonderful moments that we cherish in our lifetime.

Our exams were going on, we were giving our best, of course we don't remember what we studied now, but one thing to remember is that we used to wish each other well before writing exams. Everyone in the batch wrote their exams quickly. Rather, I used to write till the last minute, and these people used to wander here, and there enjoying, and eating after completing their exam. One day, unexpectedly everyone in the batch got miscommunication for a reason no one knows, we were not as close as previous, and slowly the gap started increasing day by day, we could see that. I don't know how it happened but one day we people had no more communication between our boys, and we girls, it was hard for all of us to ignore each other but we were so.

The last exam day was so cruel that there was an argument between me, and Sunanda. It was just a wrong communication that she was not in a position to understand me that day. She felt like I was sharing her personal information to others which I never like to do for this day even. She just asked me some random questions, and left the place without knowing what I wanted to tell her. I was left in shock, and it was painful that the only girl who understands me, left me without knowing what had actually happened. Of course, she too had her reasons, the only thing I wanted to do for her is to give the best in every possible way, sometimes we understood each other, and she understands me more than I do but few misunderstandings happen at times, and sometimes we had silence between us. Finally, we were done with exams, it means we were in the month of May, and we will be having our summer vacations.

This silence continued for hours to days, days to weeks, and weeks to months. After exams, I went to Hyderabad as I love to stay at that place because it is the place where I have my childhood memories. Those days were the first time, it was so hard because I wasn't talking to her with whom I had hours of discussion even after college. The clock used to move its seconds needle too late. When I was surrounded by my family then I was happy but when I was alone, I wondered why this happened between us. I tried to contact her to explain the things, but her anger was so high that I never got a chance to listen to her voice as long as I was in Hyderabad.

Those holidays were too long, and after a heart-drenching wait I was near to the end of the holidays so I booked my train tickets for the return journey to my hometown. I'm a kind of girl who loves to travel independently so when I was in B.Tech, I got the chance to travel alone, and it was a good experience to know how to travel alone, moreover we should be brave enough to know how to handle ourselves, and explore life. Yeah, I know for a train journey alone I'm exaggerating with these words but you know when we get some freedom while growing up in the initial days of adulting, the feeling of doing everything independently alone is high itself, I was not even in my 25s by then, I was in the middle of my teens. That's how I went to Hyderabad, and returned home with the urge to go back to college soon, and talk to her.

# 8

It was a bright morning, I got ready for college with the uniform on, and the ID tag around my neck. I was very much excited this time as it had been a month that I hadn't seen, and talked to her. I went to college after reopening, and I was probably a week late. I entered our classroom, and soon all my friends came near me, hugged, and punched me for being late, and were talking to me. I was replying to them but my eyes were scanning for her just like a scanner scans until it gets the required QR code. At that moment, she was my QR code. Once I saw her, I set my heart on her just like I received my QR code. This really happens not only for people who are in love but also for people who are in good friendship, and that heart beats more when there's a cold war happening between the two of you. She then came in, and guessed my presence there, but she didn't look at me. That feeling of avoidance gave a slap on my face, it really hurt me. I felt alone for a while, I went to her, and said "Hi", she replied "Hi", just a reply. There were two other girls sitting in the bench already where she sat, as it's our second year in college we got promoted to the $2^{nd}$ floor. The classroom had 3 columns of benches, one column for boys, the remaining two were for girls. What to do? It's just the girl population, that's it, no gender bias or anything. I sat beside Sunanda who was sitting in $2^{nd}$ column - $1^{st}$ bench, she immediately shifted to other end of the bench, I felt like the blood flow into my heart stopped for a second. I had no other option but to choose the other bench, she started to sit in the $1^{st}$ bench (which is opposite to where we sit in general) after college got reopened, and was not sitting beside the other 2 girls as well. Sravs, and Mouni were sitting in the next column $1^{st}$ bench with two more girls, I went back to them, and sat there, and from that day I started to sit away from them. It wasn't a good experience, yet I had to adjust for that. I chose the $3^{rd}$ column $2^{nd}$ bench because I had a diagonal view to see her whenever I wanted to. When the lecturer was teaching about some topic, I saw her eyes turning towards me, and when I made an immediate contact, she just took her eyes off me. It was like two love birds wanting to stay close but couldn't. I remembered our first-year lab days where we two used to sit separately as per seating arrangement. Whenever I looked at her, she somehow got to know that I was looking at her, she immediately turned back, and winked at me, this was the most touching moment that we had every time. The same thing might strike in her mind too, so she was looking at me I felt to myself. Everyone in the class came, and asked us why we were sitting apart from each other. They all got to know that we had some miscommunication between us. I tried to convince her every time when I got a chance, I missed her closeness with me, our lunch time, the fun we had, I felt a bit jealous when she was surrounded by some other friends. One of the good things about her is that from every bench at least one person was close to her. That's the good heart, and the kindness she showers on people. Slowly a month passed.

It would be a good thing if she scolded me or else she put her doubts in front of me instead she chose a silent war that left me helpless. But when I asked something or said something, she used to reply with just a reply, not less, not more. That made me go crazy thinking why she was doing that. Finally, one day Sravs said that Sunanda was planning to move from this college to the other, that word created a mini heart attack in my heart, I called her by my side, and asked her to sit for which she refused, then, I held her hand, and couldn't control my tears, that was the burden I was carrying from a month. She melted like an ice as soon as she saw the tears in my eyes, and sat beside me, I leaned my head on her shoulder, and cried out loud, "Please don't let me be alone again, if you have any anger upon me just let it out today itself but please stop doing this to me, it's hurting me the most Nandu." With these words, she started crying, and it took time for us to come back to a normal state. Later, we had our discussion, and all those misunderstandings left us. I got to know the main reason of her avoidance. It was not the misunderstanding but she knew that she would be going to a different college for some reasons, and wanted me to learn to be distant from her as every time we stick by each other's side. She thought of making me learn to be with new friends but I only had a feeling that she believed some random rumors. She was far matured, and I felt as if I'm a senseless kid in front of her without trying to know what happened even though I knew her the most. I thanked God for clearing up the silence which was a hell, and making me realize how important she is in my life, and how much more I'm supposed to know her, we had our tight group hug after a long time. At times, when a problem occurs, we shouldn't be silent. Instead, we have to solve the problem by letting the other person know what exactly happened, and what was the reason, this brings down many conflicts right away. You may think when can I understand a problem without a word, and when does the problem need to be addressed? It comes once after we go through certain phases of life's personal or other experiences.

From that day again, we started being too close to each other as if nothing happened between us, the same fun but in different places by writing small paper chits, and passing to each other but this made a bit disturbance to others for which we found a solution that only we two used to go to back bench, and sit there. Our bags used to be in the first benches apart but we sit in the back bench, and talked to each other, listened lectures, and that's how the funniest, and interesting things we had. When I was listening something very interestingly, she used to disturb me, and vice versa, we both never liked the same kind of subject, even a lecture which was very interesting to her was the lecture which I didn't get into my mind, this somehow helped us in the end of the semester while preparing for exams that we used to explain each other. The benefit I got from crying out on that day was she never left me alone, and stayed back in our college itself.

We people were talking among everyone in the batch after the boys started talking back with us when they got to know that Sunanda was moving to a different college, but it was not as good as in the beginning. For me, and Sunanda it was a bit painful yet with our bond somehow, we managed to come out of that. The next day, we had an announcement that all the students were supposed to be on the ground, and we all assembled. Every student went out with excitement as it gave us a chance to skip the classes. The ground was calm as we approached there, a green carpet was covering the barren ground, and there were some people all dressed in white making some arrangements. They didn't speak a word, silently they were doing their work, as on our HOD's (Head Of the Department) command we sat on that carpet whispering among us trying to know what was happening. Later we saw a big banner "International Yoga Day" written on it. Then we got it, and for a second, I thought to myself were we going to perform those asanas along with them or what? Soon the yoga people made us do what they came for just the way I thought, we followed them. It's quite interesting, and exciting with some of unknown moves through our body, at times, I felt as if my neck would break while doing some asanas (yoga postures). I managed to give a replica of the posture they show. I'm lean yet for some reasons I couldn't do few asanas, I thought about my other friends as they are a bit good with personality compared to me, and looked at them, while most of us were just imitating, Sunanda did all the asanas that were shown by them, and she looked pro in that, I stopped doing my asanas, and kept on looking at her with open mouth. She asked smilingly, "What, and why are you staring at me?" I closed my open mouth, took a breath, and asked her how she was doing it so smoothly, she smiled again, and said she knew them well as she used to do yoga regularly in her childhood, and mostly, she forgot it by then. I wondered if she had forgotten, and was still doing well, what if she does it regularly! It was an exclamation mark for me. The day went well with yoga.

While having workshops, and some soft skills development programs we had classes seldom, and to our delight, once we had a soft skills development program for three days. We were very excited attending the sessions, we had all branches of the college in our large auditorium. There came the trainer, a young lady who looked beautiful, and chubby, to mould us, and train on different aspects. Boys were very excited to see her, and participated in the session. She had a beautiful voice, and spoke sophisticated English, after all she is the HR in one of the FAANG MNCs. Firstly, she kept talking, and tried to make us interact with her, some of us responded while some were stuck in silence thinking what if she pointed at us, and asked a question. This sort of discomfort lies in everyone but for me, it was dominated by language as I love it. The next day, she came complaining about how she didn't get a pizza or burger in our campus, how come she gets it as it's a rural place, and is meant to be rich in its own style. We laughed at her childish innocence. She groomed us as much as she can, and the way of her pronunciation for each word with correct phonics made me learn more, and my eyes were stuck on the way she pronounced making me remember my school days in HYD, I felt happier with phonetics utterance in my ears. We people seldom spoke in English in our college though we were instructed to talk in English, the native language took its way far ahead in the race. The last day she asked us to divide into groups, and asked ten students to sit around to start group discussion on the topic she gave. I like group discussions as it gives us a chance to know how much we can acquire knowledge from others. Sunanda, and I sat next to each other followed by Sravs, and Mouni including some of our common friends, and other students such as seniors, and juniors. The topic she wanted to give was on the traditional ritual of why women should wear Mangal sutra, and several other accessories after marriage whereas men don't wear anything apart from ring on the finger. We all giggled among each other thinking about the topic. Somehow, we started, everyone stated their opinion, one stating it is our tradition, and the other saying why can't they ask men to wear them. Sunanda settled for the latter interesting subject on men to wear all the accessories, and I stuck to the first one. The discussion went on as we were the last batch in group discussion, and had sufficient time with an interesting topic in our hands, the trainer didn't stop us, encouraged us by putting additional views to elaborate on the topic standing on Sunanda's point, me with hardly two or three people continued that woman should wear them. When the topic went from Mangal sutra to difference between men, women, and reservations, later came back to the main point, I kept my point saying, "It's not only a part of tradition, it's also for the support that women require, see a woman goes through lot of hurdles from childhood, to add to them she will be separated from their maternal home, as a symbol of her parents, and husband's family, the two sutras give her enough confidence saying whatever happens now, she has one more family to support her." I don't know how far it was correct but I liked the way I spoke it in front of everyone, for which my only girl countered me saying so better to change this trend, and let men leave their home, and come to us, we are good hearted people to welcome them in." Everyone laughed, getting distracted from the serious point I kept. I too laughed for that; she raised her eyebrows asking me to counter her. This is the daily argument we have in person that now we were debating in front of everyone I thought to myself, and continued, "When our ancient people asked us to do this, there were no such questions. Our ancestors simply obeyed them without knowing the science behind it, and now we are far ahead, and have valid reasons to wear a Mangal sutra which gives potential power within, and the toe ring which touches the ground passes some energy from the earth to the body, and the ring is kept to the second toe for the regulation of a healthy menstrual cycle in women, as she goes through this every month she is supposed to wear them." Again, I was not sure whether I added a valid point in front of them or not but I personally like this culture so I can't easily give up on this topic, had it been something else, at least I would have left that but it's the power of the topic that didn't let me go though I was arguing with my friend right beside me. She appreciated my knowledge of the subject, and winked. I smiled, and she too didn't want to let go the debate, and put another point stating, "In those days women were supposed to do so much work at home but now we are ahead in everything, and have a good health so I think it's better if men carry this tradition why always 'women first' in everything? Let's give a chance to them too." She showed her sense of humour again, and the topic went on, mostly everyone gave up, and encouraged us both to argue on the topic. It was actually we did not give a chance to someone else to interfere - maybe I think I put it this way. We ran out of time after a long debate, and the trainer enjoyed our conversation like anything, she stopped us mid-way, and gave a biased judgement stating it depends on individual opinion, and both the opponents have valid points. In the end, she came to us, and asked, "Are you both best friends?" We smiled looking at each other, she got her answer, and told everyone, "While having a group discussion never ever you people choose to sit beside your besties as it won't give an end, and you people keep on arguing without closing it." She completed her sessions successfully, and left, the day ended but not the topic. When we have time, and there's no topic to discuss we discussed this, and gave our best. Though she loves the culture, it's just she wanted to give it a different perspective when she argues with me.

# 9

The more the days were moving forward the more our friendship grew. We go to college daily and if on any day we felt like not going then a day before we used to talk about that, and later, we stayed at home spending time with family. Sunanda has such a beautiful heart that she could never tell a lie, especially when she makes an eye contact. She's a brave girl. When I remember some moments, I get to know those things. In the evening, while going back home, and looking out the window, I always thought of our fun, and laughed out loud. I remembered a day that was very special. It was women's day, we were in our first year, all the students were asked to assemble in a nearby college hence we followed. It was a big college named as TP engineering college which had a very big auditorium, it was completely filled with lots of students, and staff over there, and we people were included in that, we four girls were sitting in last row because we left our class late, it's not that we were working on something, it's just our habit of being late, by the time- we entered the auditorium some guests were giving speeches, as usual we kept on talking, and playing in the last row. They asked if anyone wanted to speak a few words. I heard that, and said, "Sunanda, now you have to go there, and talk" she asked me, "Are you serious?" "Yes I am." I replied, and said, "You can talk, I know about you, just give your best." Without a second thought she stood up, all were looking at her. I was surprised if she was really going there or just leaving the room. She crossed thousands of students sitting in front of us, occupied the dais, greeted everyone, and started to speak about women empowerment. I tell you that she was the girl who spoke more than the guests sitting over there. The words that she used; the way she spoke about women kept everyone so silent that even people who were not interested to listen also got involved in that. She added some beautiful words that as of today if I close my eyes, and remember I can see her wearing a white dress speaking in front of people. Frankly, she was attracting everyone's eyes, and my eyes stuck on her thinking from where she got that much courage to speak.

While giving her speech she even added a sense of humour that made everyone in the college remember her. She said, "My legs are shivering just to reach this place but we all should get confidence within us so that women can never be underestimated by anyone. Just leave the fear out, be brave, and be bold, let the world think of you as anything but remember you have to be judged by your own selves, and not by others, just do things right, and in a sacred way. Speak up girls, it's the time. Be a speaker when someone's ears are ready to hear, and be a good listener when their mouth is opened. Be independent, work on yourself, progress, and achieve what you dreamt of." This was a bit I remembered; I had a recording of that, one day I lost the video unfortunately.

When she was getting down the stage everyone started shouting, whistling, and clapping for her beautiful message but I was just frozen, and drops of tears were rolling down my cheeks with joy. She came near me, gave me a hug, and asked me, "Did I say anything wrong?" "Just look at the response, and you only said just do anything, and don't think what others say." I said, she immediately replied, "I really don't need other people's opinion just yours because you are my one girl who supports me, and will be with me every time." I still remember the moment that our eyes were glowing with happiness.

In the evening, I called our aunty just to let her know her daughter's courage, she said she used to give speeches from her school age, aunty asked me how did she speak, what all happened, and then I got to know that it's not my words that made her talk but her inner feeling, and see she gave me the entire credit as if she spoke just because of my inspiration. She always used to give her best to her loved one's without any second thought. This simplicity gave her a special position in everyone's heart.

That day I got to know her heart some more, what's there in her mind, how she could give happiness to others, and all those small things that the world didn't know about her. When she loves a person, she would love with her entire heart, and can never lie to that person. Her kindness, her love, her empathy towards others that I never found a person with such a pure hearted soul. With these great personalities of hers, the kid in her heart loves teddies a lot. I used to think it's just her like but later, I realised they make her feel happier, and express herself to them at least as she couldn't do with humans who mostly hurt her.

After getting to know day by day more about her, at times I even got a respect towards her that I can't show but in the form of my love towards her I can show that. Even I don't know all the things, and hidden feelings in her when we had a fight but the day I read her diary made me realize that she is something more that I have to know in deep. During fights, I initially thought she might have a negative impression that she shouted upon me but the truth was very interesting that she just wanted to protect me from being bad in other's perspective, and I realized my mistakes. I'm the one who is very close to her still, at times I fail to understand her, and imagine how could a person like stranger understands her inner beauty was my every time doubt for which she replied, "I'll be just good to a person who loves me, and even to a person who wants to hurt me, being good just makes us happy within. I won't lose anything right?" Now, there was a brake on the bus as my stop arrived, and it was a break for my thoughts too, I smiled within, and went home.

# 10

I don't know what all we used to talk in our classroom. There were times when our lecturers asked us to keep quiet, and listen to the class. Once we reached college; we used to talk, when the class was going on; we used to talk, during lunch breaks, bio breaks, labs, practical exams; we talked, library a place where everyone is expected to be silent there also we whispered, and continued to talk, after getting into the bus through mobiles we chatted, we talked after reaching home, and at evenings until night we fell asleep we used to talk. People around us, Sravs, and Mouni, always used to ask us what do we discuss, and how long does it last. We two looked at each other, and were not sure what the hell around the world we discussed but we used to keep on doing the same. From mid of second year onwards, we started to sit in the first bench together. We thought, "Why can't we do the same things just like we were on the last bench?" So, we had our fun, eating snacks, throwing chits on Mouni, and Sravs asking them to reply, when they don't care about us, and listen to the lecture, it would make us more arrogant, and we used to threaten them in a funny manner, not only we two, later the girls sitting beside us also enjoyed our company. We planned to go here, and there, by the end of the day it resulted in canceling all the plans. A memorable thing is that we never used to blame anyone, rather Sunanda, and I stood in front of each other, and gave a sarcastic look by gesturing in our code language because we knew those plans won't workout.

Whenever we both had a quarrel, and sat apart from each other, our lecturers used to question if there was any fight between us, it was a wonder for them to see us like that. Mostly, we never had a clash on each other's behavior but we always had a fight regarding some of our friends with the way that we treat them, and were we being good to them or not, our ultimate agenda is the same to see all our friends happy but we had different ideas that brought a clash. I remember up to this day, we never had a fight for our behavioral changes or attitude differences because we remained same which is the best thing.

When she had a bad day, she used to talk less. Soon after I entered the classroom with her body language, I used to tell myself that she was happy today or she was in a bad mood. She couldn't express her inner feelings to anyone else except me that even if she had pain inside her she used to fake a smile that others think she's happy but I can realize whether it's from her heart or it just appeared for others happiness. If a person hurts her, she just used to be good to that person when asked I get an answer, "At least by hurting me if a person gets happiness, I'm ready to get hurt so that other person can be happy." This made me furious, I used to say better you stay away from those people, instead she said, "How could I do that after all those are the people whom I care about." I feel how could she be so nice to others even if someone tries to hurt her. I really don't know whether to praise her for her kindness towards others or to stop her from doing that.

Till this day I can say that if I meet our college friends, and ask about Sunanda there is zero student to talk rude about her. She's a kind of girl that even haters would love her when they come to know about her. That's my girl.

Days started moving forward quickly and we were at the end of our second year, that was one more attached year, there's an emotional connection growing up more. I really didn't remember the fight, but we again had a big fight that we stopped talking for more than a week. Now, if I recollect that she used to be a kid while we were having a fight, she come to class alone, and sit very distinct from me, wouldn't have a direct eye contact to me, sits apart during lunch, and she uses the most powerful weapon that she got surrounded by others ignoring me that made me gone crazy, and my jealous rate reaches its crest. One Saturday evening, I decided to go to her home, and make her cool down. Sunday morning, I woke up, got ready, and went to her home along with our gang to get our misunderstandings clear altogether so that we could be the same as we were in the first year. We all gathered at her home. I remember she became angry at seeing all the people around her, and from the other side she was about to cry. I took her hands in mine, we were trying to get off from that quarrel, and in the meanwhile by bringing the first year's fight in the conversation, everyone became rageous. We got to know it was getting worse, and we were losing control of our words. I was more worried that it would end up with our fight again, and without thinking further, I fell on my knees in front of Sunanda which led to a great silence. I said no anger should last more, and we are friends, it's a beautiful relationship, and I can't think a second of losing you as a friend, let's stop this, and be as good as we were. She melted again that she couldn't control her tears, and sobered by sitting down, soon Sravs, and all sat down beside us, and we were crying as if we were in an emotional Telugu film scene. I tell you it's a funny moment as of now if I think about it, but that day it was then we realized again how much we mean in each other's lives. We all got set after a while, and had lunch, making fun of each other, and all making fun the way I fell on my knees. Even this time Mouni didn't show up, she spoiled the plan to meet altogether. But we called her on the phone, and as usual told her everything which made her feel happy. Sunanda later scolded me for felling on my knees in front of her. "Never you dare do that again." I laughed, and we continued with our fun.

Without doing anything for her she used to care about me, and gave me the best place in her heart. Even after the quarrel, she hadn't shown any difference, she used to be as good as she was before. This is such an inner beauty in her that even after hurting her she never replaced the position in her heart. I really love that beauty in her which is known less to others and more to me.

# 11

Every time if something is wrong, Sunanda used to avoid that talk but I struggled to get to know what's going on. She all of sudden became weak, and again energetic. We didn't know what that was but she became so scared at those times. Later after several months she talked about her health that she had thyroid. She too got to know about that then, which affected her health badly, and that was the time she mostly became weak.

She fought against thyroid so strongly, and had developed a great mindset to overcome its side effects. People think thyroid is common these days but the person who gets it knows the pain. The person gains weight, and loses weight, hormonal imbalance, excessive heat, and several other things affects, it differs for individual. We all encouraged her to be strong enough but it was her own pain, and her own health condition that we could just give moral support only, she's the one to deal physically, and mentally. But you know when a person suffers internally due to physical or mental pain, there should always be at least a single person to walk beside him/her to give some external guts to face the difficulties. She has her own family, and we friends are there to cheer her up that made her come out of the pain not at that instance but slowly. She used to have a regular check-up for that, and somehow, she managed herself.

We both used to go out mostly, and had fun. Sometimes Sravs, and Mouni used to join us. But Sravs is such a scared girl that she won't come out just like a tortoise hides in its shell. She always has thousands of doubts running in her mind, she won't understand everything so quick, and keep on asking us what's the thing that we people were talking, and laughing, when related to studies her brain works so sharp than us, coming to Mouni she's a fire brand even if we just call her name to ask something, she responds with a great base voice which made her angry bird among our four girls. We always had a conference call. It began with me, and her having a conversation then we added Sravs, and Mouni, had a long conversation, and after they both hang-up the call we both continued our talk, and finally ended after more than an hour. This became our every time conference code that every time either

Sunanda or I started a call, continued with them, and ended with our two conversations.

Once we were in the class, it was afternoon after lunch break, Sunanda was talking something but I was in my imaginary world thinking about something very deep. She called me, and was telling something that they only reached my ears, but not my mind, she looked at me, and just gave a slap on my face. It was like a shock that she too neither expected that the slap would be so strong nor even I. There was a pin drop silence in the class because it was the sleepy time, and we all had enough food then only, and listening a class after lunch is like playing a slow background music, and making us fall asleep, this sound resonated at its extent. Everyone laughed looking at us, and we both fell on the bench, and laughed. Our lecturer stopped speaking, and asked what happened, none of the students spoke a word, he continued the class again. Later, she felt so bad that she thought she hurt me with the sudden slap but actually it was a good memory that made the whole class burst into laughter, and that's not painful anyways. Every single moment can be captured into its beautiful frames that I have with her.

I always had a wish to visit Tirupati, offer my prayers, and to see the beauty of it. Once, unexpectedly I visited the place as one of my childhood friends was going there along with her friends, and out of all the members one girl canceled her plan so, they asked me to join as it was my wish too. It was a one-week trip, we traveled via train, and I was very excited that my wish was coming true. We enjoyed the train journey by singing songs, telling stories, and having fun by playing dumb charades where we are supposed to guess the movie name with gestures given by one person. The next day early in the morning, we reached Tirupati railway station, seeing the place with hills around, and fog, we were in a state of euphoria, and tranced by its beauty. We can see one of the mountains appear as the Lord Venkateshwara Swamy, we visited the temple the next day. We waited in the queue for a long time, and it was midnight when we reached inside the temple. The moment I saw the idol, all the pain just vanished or might be the happiness that I felt which made me forget the restlessness up till then. We took as many laddus as possible, these laddus have a very unique taste. We can't even define them. A small bite of laddu gives inner tranquility. We visited all the nearby temples over there, and for food there is a free service named Vengamamba in which thousands of people get served daily with proper quality, and the food has good taste. The place looked very royal, and the people who do service are so kind to everyone who comes in. After visiting most of the places, and temples, one evening before leaving we went for shopping where I bought a beautiful pair of bangles for us, and a watch for me as the watch Sunanda gave me stopped working. Going back to college, I showed all the things I bought for everyone. Sunanda loved the bangles which I bought so we decided to have half-half for both of us. They looked more beautiful on her hands than mine. The watch I had on my left hand was always dotted by her pen unintentionally so I decided to put my watch on my right hand as she sits close to my heart, from then till this day I got habituated to put the watch on my right wrist. The bangles that I gave her always stick to her hand, and every year I used to bring her beautiful bangles that looked more beautiful when she wore them.

# 12

Another nice afternoon, there were no classes going on by that time, we all were chit chatting with each other, and Sunanda said, "When we get our degree in our hands, and get settled in our future, one day let's buy our houses beside each other so that we can stay close enough even after getting married, let's make our husbands know our friendship, and make them a part of our friendship then comes our children, and they grow up together, be as good friends as we are, goes to the same school, and college, and it repeats a loop further." She kept on imagining in that beautiful world, with my smile she came out of that, and asked me why I was looking at her like that, for a second, I really enjoyed that feeling of chain bond moving towards future generations. We laughed together because of the madness. But it's a heart touching moment.

In class, we would frequently jot down notes while listening to lectures, most of which were simply pen marks crossing through our books. She is a good artist she can draw anything on free hand that just looked perfect, and I'm a girl who doesn't even know how to draw the mountains, and the sunrise perfectly which is the basic drawing we learn in our early school days, even in my B.Tech drawing exams I got stamp marks. I loved the way that she drew everything which eventually created an active interest in me to learn how to draw, as of now I can draw few things not that perfect but they would be nice as she made me learn few tricks to draw like firstly to draw an outline, and then concentrate on what you are seeing or imagining. This is how her passion, and interests attracted me, and made me learn things, we both like to do crafts, mostly she does. She herself made beautiful earrings of 2-3 pairs, and gifted them to me with no occasion. If she likes something she will ask me to buy them or do them for her, though very small with lots of love. Sometimes it's not the thing that you present, it's just the love, and care that you shower, makes the difference.

We felt that our bond towards each other made us distant from our friends as we used to engage in ourselves which sometimes brought some clashes among our friends. But we enjoyed even the friendly jealousy. All have their own world with family or other friends but when it comes to us, we have a world where we could speak everything regarding all our families, and friends, and mostly our silence spoke many words that made a slight difference from others. Whenever I feel like something or some incident is going to hurt her, I myself put a step forward and hide those things from her, this actually made her angry at times. Later, when she got to know she used to ask me the reasons, for the upcoming days she realized, and stopped asking me rather she understood that whatever I do, I'll do for her happiness. This is the most sensitive thing because I'm a girl who can take anything so easy but she's so sensible that every little thing hurts her a lot, and she doesn't want anyone to know the pain behind her smile.

She always gave me true happiness whereas I sometimes used to hide the truth, and never let her knew few things because that truth of people's fake personalities would let her down. If the truth is getting suppressed for the sake of good, it's better to hide it. I want to see her happy so I let her be happy as much as possible in our world. A girl who makes everyone happy has the right to be happier than others but mostly I saw her to be dull, sad, and think about something in herself.

She is a kind of girl who hates tea whereas I was an addicted person for that, without chai my day won't get started. From my childhood, I had this habit of drinking the tea made by my dad the minute I open my eyes. He even took me to famous tea stalls in Hyderabad in the evenings when I act to be sad, he made me drink Irani chai with Osmania biscuits which is famous, and I loved that combination though the saddest part is the biscuit drinks more than me, I showed some mercy on it. I was shocked when I got to know that neither she nor her family members have the habit of drinking tea. Her main requirement from her future husband was he should have no habit of drinking tea. This was another shock that the majority of the people throughout the world have a habit of drinking tea or coffee, and how come she would get a husband who has no such habit. I satirically used to say he must be a tribal person actually no, even tribes have the habit of drinking at least tea leaves water.

# 13

Most of the time I used to visit Hyderabad during vacations or family festivals. It was once during November month I had to come to Hyderabad with my mom because of our family pooja, so we planned to book tickets, and all were set. I told Sunanda about our visit to Hyderabad. She became so pale, and asked me to stay in their home, and let my mom go. "But I have to go." I replied, which really disappointed her. We reached Hyderabad, and we were a little busy in those event's preparation. I thought about her how could she manage without me in the college, I used to call her everyday especially during lunch time not to let her be alone while eating, she sometimes broke into tears that she really missed me a lot, and uploaded status saying, "Why should I think of a girl who left me but I don't know why tears are shedding from my eyes while I'm typing this" which made me feel sad looking at those lonely status waiting for me, and asking me to come back soon, meet her, and stick beside her. Again, she herself regained after some time, and talked well. You know we girls with mood swings.

We had our family pooja done so great and it was a memorable day for our family, we had fun that all our relatives, and cousins attended the pooja. We returned home after few days. When I went back to college, she saw me from upstairs, and soon ran fast, gave me a tight hug, and bursted into tears without a word. That hug told me how badly she missed me though she was surrounded by all our friends. She mostly looks so strong but the truth is she's more emotional, especially because she can't bear the thought of being far away from her loved ones.

When we were free in college, we used to go Bobbili, went for shopping, and explored around because we don't remember the routes, we used to walk round, and round to reach our destination every time. As of today, I can remember every point of those streets that we roamed together, and how funny, and beautiful memories we had at every place. We both mostly loved roadside food. We bought all the food items that we wanted, and walked counting our footsteps saying that our steps will move together every time. People think these words are meant for lovers but no, you can ask any two besties they usually have these kinds of conversations every single time.

The very first film we all girls watched together was Mahanubhavudu Telugu film, we don't remember how funny the movie was but we only remembered the entertainment that we made while watching the film, frankly speaking we haven't watched the movie completely, we all were thinking about some funny incidents in college, discussing that, and laughing all together. Sravs was like "Arre yaar, what you guys are doing? Let's enjoy the film first, we paid for the tickets na? This entertainment we can have in college as well, why to pay for the movie?" for that we countered by having a discussion out of the box, and she became curious to know what happened, we replied to her the same with which she initially came up. When there's a gang of friends sitting, and talking, even a minute thing they discuss, makes them feel as if it was the funniest thing that happened in that year, and no other comedy can beat it. In all those 4 years we just watched only 3 films. It's not because we won't watch, it's because every time we planned, we failed, and these 3 movies were unplanned so we watched them all of a sudden which added a few more memories into our diaries.

Sunanda loved watching reality shows whereas I used to be a bit far from that. I rarely used to watch movies or any other shows but this girl watched the Big Boss Telugu show every season without missing a single episode. She admired one personality in every season, and used to vote for that person. She even had a discussion with some other classmates about what happened in the last episode. I used to look at their faces as I don't know the show even though my two uncles are the cameramen in that show. Having an interest to watch or not is an individual interest so I paid less attention to that, she never forced me to watch as she knows me.

# 14

After not celebrating the first birthday well in college, my parents later on used to take me to Vizag, and we visit a temple at Anakapalli, the temple is known for Nookambika Devi (goddess Durga ma), and they used to make my day happy, and feel blessed, this happened for other two years, everyone used to call me at night, and wished me but not Sunanda, she wished me at around 10 am or else she takes even more of her sweet time. For those two years while I was traveling on the bus, she wished me with full energy that I could feel her warmth in those wishes, and she felt a bit bad as I was not with her, and later said, “It's okay, for today you stay, and enjoy with your family, and the remaining 364 days we will be together” by cheering herself up. I remember how surprisingly Sunanda celebrated my B.Tech final year birthday. We didn't go to temple in that year because Sunanda wanted me to be with her as it was our final year, with a lot of argument, and conversation with her, managing my parents we canceled our trip, I decided to go to college on that year as my parents told me, "Be with your friends for this day, we shall plan again." At night, some of my friends wished me except her. She never thought of wishing me first at sharp 12 o' clock as everyone does, at least in my B.Tech final year. She called me in the morning around 7am, and I hate to wake up early so she tried to annoy me every day by calling at 6am in the morning, and asks, "Are we going to college today?" I get frustrated with this question that, "Last night we had the same discussion so why do you ask the same thing again?" she says, "Just for confirmation", and hangs up the call. Just like every day she called me in the morning, and let her mother, and sister wish me, and after that I expected that she was going to wish me but she never did, instead she said "Ok, let's meet in the college" which made me a bit disappointed. While going to college she called me, and said, "We are at Bobbili temple just come here, and we'll go to the temple first." so I did. All my friends came to me, hugged me, and wished me. It was one of my bench mate's birthday too, I wished her back, and looked at Sunanda as my eyes always search her first, she was standing a meter away, and said, "Now can we go in?" I was angry at her this time, she won't wish me instead she asked me to come to college, and made me cancel my trip. We went in, took darshan, and stayed there for a while after taking selfies, while going back, she asked all my friends to go to college, and we will be back within an hour, so all did, and I asked her where were we going, she asked me to follow her, and while we were walking, she said, "Why you didn't get ready much, you are looking too simple, look at the other girl she is completely dolled up." I just smiled back. We reached a bakery in which she ordered two pastries for me, and gave me to eat them because I love pastries, and she completely hates that taste, she was standing a bit far because she doesn't like that smell but just to make me eat, she was there concealing her feelings. I understood that, and asked the shopkeeper to pack them so that I can eat them later. She took me to a bangle store, and bought bangles. I said no but she didn't listen to me. Just to make her friend look good in everyone's eyes, she bought some beautiful bangles of orange color that matched my simple birthday dress, and she herself put those bangles on me yet she didn't wish me while presenting that. After making me look good completely we both reached college. It was our mid exams, we were having an online test in the morning, and a written test in the afternoon that time. We were done with the exam, and in the evening Sunanda, Sravs, and Mouni celebrated my friend's, and my birthday by making us cut the cake, presenting small gifts, and we all have a frame in our homes with a big photo of birthday one's, and all small photos of our B.Tech memories. We were enjoying that moment by smearing cake, and still she didn't say happy birthday which gave me an urge to ask her, "Why don't you just wish me instead you do all these things, I just need a small heartful wish from you." In return she replied, "This is a special day as you were born but I can't give all my love only for this day, and be quite, and normal for the remaining days, you are special to me just as special as this day, and for every day, this celebration I'm doing today is because we are not that rich to cut a cake everyday right! so only some days I make you to do this." She chuckled, and these true, and straight forward words made me feel high. At the end she held my hand, and presented me with one more gift. I was opening that thinking of what could it be, my eyes were on the gift, and her eyes on me. I unwrapped the cover, and couldn't believe what I was holding in my hands. I was completely in love with that gift, it was a small wooden guitar with the head having one of our beautiful pictures in which she was sitting on my lap. Below that picture was written "Happy birthday to my lovely Hima." I like guitars much, and always thought of buying one, previously when we went out, in a photo studio I saw a guitar that was on the wall, I held it, and was looking at that, Mouni was grabbing my pictures when holding that, Sunanda just looked at me as if I was insane, and said, "Let's go else the shopkeeper charges us more." But I never thought that she already decided, and planned to gift me one day. As we were still studying she said, "I can afford this for you now but one day when I earn money, I'm going to present you the real one, Happy birthday Hima." Not for the gift, not for the future gift, the last words wishing me made me excited, and those words filled me completely apart from all those gifts. That guitar was one of the best presentations from her in my life. She hugged me, and whenever she feels extremely delighted tears roll down her cheeks, and that was the moment tears were running as heavy as floods. She said, "This is the last birthday of yours that we are celebrating together, and from next year onwards you'll be at some other place, and I'll be at some other place right!" There was silence for a while. We held each other's hand, and just prayed that our bond would remain the same until our last breath. Then I realized she wished me the birthday wishes as purely as her tears were coming from her eyes, and I couldn't find words to complete that moment.

# 15

One fine day, it was Sravani's sister's engagement, and she invited all our friends to attend the function. However, as usual, a planned one couldn't be succeeded, so only I went to Parvathipuram. I got dressed up in a pink long top dress with its neck part highlighted by beautiful white embroidery. Sunanda was waiting for me at the complex. She picked me up, dressed in a simple yet elegant way, wearing a beautiful light orange-colored long top complemented with a gold chain around her neck. Overall, she looked cute, and decent. She had a good level of melanin, which made her look beautiful in her own brown-toned skin, her true beauty shone in her eyes, giving a great charm to her face. Color is just a skin tone, but true beauty lies within, and she's a beauty inside, and out.

We both went to a nearby gift store, bought a gift, and then reached Sunanda's home. Our aunt, and our cute little sister welcomed me with a hug, we got ready to go to the function hall. Aunty treated me equally with her two daughters, making us look good with some added ornaments. The three of us reached the venue, and greeted everyone. On normal days, Sravs looked beautiful in her cute way, and that day she was looking even more beautiful, and elegant. She was the main attraction after the bride, and groom. She wore a beautiful half saree, adorned with enough jewelry to complement her looks, and with a red rose a bit close to her left ear in her loose hair made her look ravishing. We teased her that she would find her groom at that engagement party itself, and she giggled with a blush at the thought of getting married.

There was an anchor who initially asked everyone to dance. When people hesitated a bit, she forcefully set them on the dance floor, and made the event lively. That was the first-time we girls were dancing together, despite not knowing how to dance perfectly, I managed to have fun. When you are happy, there's no need to dance a perfect step; you can move your hands, and legs randomly, and so I did. Sunanda, our little sister, and Sravs were good enough in dance. *My* girl also knew Bharatanatyam; she was well-trained from her childhood, and had some presentations in that field.

I met Sunanda's, and Sravani's common childhood friends there, they talked to me so nicely. Later, Sravs got busy welcoming the guests. Sunanda, her childhood friends, our sister, and I were sitting together in a round conference, discussing all sorts of funny things. For a while, I felt a bit jealous when some of her friends were being so close to her. I don't know why, but I felt so. It's not only a boy who gets jealous of a girl; in every relation, when we feel possessive of a person, we experience jealousy. However, one thing brought a smile to my face – she was completely enjoying that moment. I could see her wet eyes; as whenever she laughs heartily, her eyes become wet. She looked at me, and gave a smile to make me feel comfortable. I felt those people would be with her for some time, and the remaining days she would be with me. One thing was clear – no matter how many people she stayed with, she would always look for me, so there was no need to be so possessive.

After having lunch, and enjoying ourselves there, we left the place in evening. As planned earlier, I decided to stay at Sunanda's home. So, we went back home, and that was the first time I was staying at her place. We got relaxed; uncle came, and took us to a nearby ice-cream parlor where both the sisters go regularly. Later, in the late evening, she prepared mixture – she goes to the kitchen sometimes, and as I was there, she decided to prepare it for me. She is, of course, a good cook. At night, we had dinner from outside, all the four family members were so close to me, trying to make me feel at home. I really enjoyed their company. Later, we three girls went upstairs, and watched TV. Actually, the TV was on, and we were cracking jokes among each other. Both of them felt so happy that I was there with them. I could see that in their eyes. Suddenly, Srija came to me, and kissed my forehead so affectionately. I was a bit surprised; she said, "Thanks for being there with my sister. She always speaks about you, and how you both enjoy each other's company." I was glad that from then on, I was having an extended family who takes care of me, and treats me as equal as their daughter, sister. We thought of staying awake all night, doing this, and that; however, we were so tired that we couldn't resist ourselves, and fell asleep around 12 at night. Sunanda has a habit of sleeping with her spectacles on. While having them on, she falls asleep, and later any of the three would take them off. She looked so innocent, especially while she was sleeping, she looked so peaceful, and calm. I smiled inside, and closed my eyes. The next day we woke up around 11 am. Only we three were there; aunt, and uncle went on duty.

I forgot to bring my toothbrush, so Sunanda, and I went for a small walk to buy it. While walking, she told me about all the places she had memories of in those streets. After getting ready, and having our breakfast, Sunanda took me to some of her favorite neighbors' places where she spent her childhood. She showed me all the houses, the people that she's surrounded by, and even the roads she had memories of when she was a kid. I simply loved her beautiful family, surroundings, and everything that she told me.

Sunanda loves carving, designing, and crafts. She is a multi-talented girl. I saw all her interior designing in her home, how beautifully she decorated everything. I sometimes feel how come she's so talented in every field, and in the best way, she's a good painter too. All these made me try to do, and learn from her. After seeing her daily, I just gave it a try, and got better. I can do art crafts well, which I learned from her. However, she never forced her hobbies on me. If I asked her, she would tell me, because she believed that everyone has their own hidden talent, and that mustn't be public every time; sometimes it should be comfortable for the individual. She had such kind of well-mannered behavior.

Later, in the afternoon, I prepared to leave but these girls were not letting me go. However, I too wanted to stay, but I couldn't as I had to go home soon since my parents were waiting for me. I gave some chocolates to my little sister, and left the place. Sunanda came along with me up to the complex; we were feeling happy, we could see that in each other's eyes. On the way, she took me to the school where she studied. We went in, and she showed me her classroom, and told some memories that she had in that school. Then I left the place which was a bit hard for both of us because we knew that day would never come back again. Thinking about all these beautiful moments, I didn't realize when I reached my place, as I was staring outside the window, and just feeling those moments of true happiness, and then there was a brake on the moving bus, and on my thoughts too. I got down, and went home.

Back in college, after classes when we had time left, we used to go to Bobbili for shopping, and buy some ladies stuff. As I said earlier, we started at a point, roamed here and there to reach the same place where we started. It's not because we want to do so but somehow, we missed the road. For this with our intelligence we used to coat it up saying the road missed us, and we were straight the way ahead. When Mouni, and Sravs were with us, we never had such an experience; it's only when we left together. In return, we used to halt at a place near auto stand to drink lassi which was special item of that place, we three drank lassi whereas Sunanda ends up drinking lemon water. When I asked her the reason, she simply said I like lemon water more than lassi, savouring the flavor of sour lemon taste. Every Friday during lunch most of the students in college used to eat biryani which was brought by one seller on bike, we used to like that biryani so much as it's only once in a week we got that bike biryani, and remaining days we used to keep on thinking when would that uncle come again so that we can eat our favorite food.

# 16

We had a habit of doing Dubsmash just like Instagram reels, later Dubsmash was replaced with TikTok; however, it was banned later. These were some of the more memorable moments we had. Sunanda liked to do that with me. Later, I got interested, so we decided to start recording one afternoon, only me, and Sunanda were doing that TikTok. We used Sravani's phone for good camera quality, Mouni recorded the video, and we both performed like real actors. That was in our minds so much that we used to have hours of discussion to do this, and that, the latest videos, whatever we felt interested in. It was not even one take; the TikTok video span is hardly 30 seconds, and we used to take hours to get a perfect one. Mostly, we used to laugh in the middle, which made Mouni angry, and she refused to record the video, we used to request her, and Sravs. As of now, when I hear those songs, I can feel our movements, and expressions in front of my eyes, even with the dressing colors we had that day, that's how much they affected us, remembering how we enjoyed those moments. At times, we had a serious argument that ended in a bit of disappointment, and the next day we again thought of a new video. After completing every video in the evening, we used to upload status on WhatsApp, and our friends obviously made comments, however the performance was. I know we are not great actors, but we filled our hearts completely with joy while doing that. They are such beautiful clips, and expressions that we cry out of laughter by seeing, and remembering the background bloopers.

Again, after a year, me, and my mom went to Hyderabad as it was my uncle's marriage, and this time as usual Sunanda became so low that she couldn't let me go away from her but I had to. I had to go through our college but the bus won't stop there so I packed some chocolates in a cover, and left the change in that cover, I called them, and asked them to wait at the college entrance gate so they came, soon the bus is crossing the college I threw that cover, and they held it, some were fallen down, she just looked at me waving her hand. Days were passing, this time she was a bit strong or else she pretended so, she enjoyed with all other girls, took selfies, did TikTok, and sent those videos to me to tease me, and of course I felt a bit jealous, and yes, I was happy just because she was trying to get into something so that she can't be alone. When I came back after a month, they didn't even come down. Those people who came down running, gave me a hug, and welcomed me back a year ago were not there. I couldn't hear their yelling. I entered the class, other classmates greeted me, and asked how I spent my holidays. While replying to them, I received a message notification saying come out, it was from Sunanda, I smiled, and came out to the corridor. No one was there, I was searching. Soon I received another pop-up saying come upstairs so I went upstairs thinking what these people were doing, then I saw Sravs, and Mouni. They both came, and hugged me but my eyes were completely searching for Sunanda, then she entered which made me feel blessed, she was recording a video. Then we hugged after beating each other. That video looks quite funny that her eyes were filled with tears after seeing me a month later. This is how every time she made my day, and we had plenty of memories that are as high as possible.

# 17

SMSB: This is not a simple thing; it means our four years of B.Tech memories that last for a lifetime. Sravani Mounika Sunanda Bindu. We just wrote it as every gang does in their college life, but we did something more; whenever we had a pen, pencil, or even chalk in our hands, we used to write SMSB. It brought us some inner happiness, which made our days filled with positive vibes. Likewise, we used to write on our books, benches, walls, and even on the washroom doors. We made those letters look bright to have a view from afar. We wrote on our backs some crazy crush names, and the remaining three would guess. It was quite interesting, we laughed after figuring them out. Sunanda had great handwriting. Whatever she writes, the look will change, and the word itself will be beautiful. That's how her writing was. Most of our handwritings are similar, but her writing has something more attractive than mine.

Today, too, I can see her writing style in mine. Maybe because we were always together, our writing styles also synced. The funniest thing was that whenever we bunk our classes, we used to hide in our bus, and write even on that bus window. We cracked jokes on each other. Everyone says that a backbencher has the best life, but as the students from back benchers to first-benchers, we have seen all sorts of fun, educational values, and tremendous change within. We still maintain all kinds of energy levels when we are together. We had a mini canteen in our desks, and sometimes we were even caught by our lecturers because of the tasty smell. If we wanted to talk to each other, we simply wrote a small note in our books. At the end of the semester, when we opened our books to read, we mostly saw the conversation we had but not the subject, and we called, and scolded each other funnily, saying, "Should I write this conversation in the exams?" The other would say, "Yeah, you write this, and you will never get a B.Tech certificate."

In every semester we used to like a subject so much that even if we didn't want to listen to it, it still went straight into our brains. That was the major advantage we had when our exams were near. At night or in the evening, we had a conference call, and discussed the subject so well that we could give a direct attempt, and gain the best score. The conversation used to be so funny, with education involved. B.Tech is not completed unless you savor the taste of backlogs. In every student's life, there would be at least one backlog that might be due to not attempting well, attempting still failed because of the wrong evaluation that we feel or at least because of a health issue that the person couldn't attempt the exam, and of course there are chances that some people do pass without a single backlog in exams; those are God's gifted children, we used to say. All these things happened in our lives too, and we can proudly say that we too had backlogs. One has to experience that taste of sweet, and sour to add beauty to life. I'm very bad at Maths, I don't know why but from my childhood that subject brought me a lot of confusion, fear, and some ignorance that I can understand another subject but not this one. In B.Tech, we will be having Maths only during our first year, and my subject that I couldn't clear was also Maths but still I cleared it up in my first supplementary exam that I could proudly say as of now. That was the backlog I had along with physics, actually I like this subject yet failed but I gave a good attempt in the exam, and achieved my best whereas my friends also had different ones, and they also cleared them soon, even the topper

Sravs also had a backlog that was just because her health condition was not good by that time, as I said these would be the main reasons that one could have a backlog, and that failure experience is also a good thing since from childhood we never had a failure in any subject but then we had a failure, and we managed ourselves for the next semester by knowing the loop holes like analysing how the paper could be, and how we should attempt, that's how we discussed well, and never failed again. See, togetherness can make one succeed even in life. If we get a hurdle or a failure, we must have the capability to share it at least with a single person to get to know the loopholes, how to work on it later, and the ways to face the problems. Life is as simple as those B.Tech semesters. If we fail, we still get opportunities, but one has to know how to handle the problem, and how to solve it. If we fail on the first attempt, are we going to lose our hopes, and stop writing for the next time? No, right! So, if we can't give up on a four-year educational certificate, how can we give up on these beautiful 100 years of life? We can't get back those memories or moments, right? Just be focused on life. If you fail, still give life an opportunity to knock at your door. We even have an advanced supplementary in B.Tech, and as for life, we have more, and more. Just get to know them. If alone you can't find a solution to a problem, just allow at least a single person who's important to you to have the opportunity to enter your life. I do know sayings can be easier, and facing would be tough; believe me, experiencing life can make those statements come true in reality.

# 18

Every girl has a male bestie in her life. I too have a friend with whom I can share every feeling without a second thought, and that man has been in my life since the 8th grade. I made him my friend ever since I met him, but he never had that much of a friendly talk with me. The thing is, every time it doesn't work out, you feel a person as your bestie, and the other person should also do the same. Sometimes you just have to care without any expectations, then only you can give your best. When expectations start automatically one day or another, you get an urge, and demand to receive. This person is Srinu, my all-time good friend. During our 9th grade, I don't know why, but he stopped talking to me, and I used to plead to him like anything to talk to me or just say a 'hi', and 'bye' in a day at least. I used to pray to God at times to let him talk to me, but it was never done. One day, we completed our high school studies, but still he didn't talk to me. Coming to me, I'm like glue if I treat someone as my friend; I don't give up on him/her so easily. I used to learn about him, how he was, and where he was from one of my friends.

Years passed, and I had a soft corner for him, but that doesn't mean I used to think about him every time. When I was in my B.Tech, I unexpectedly got a friend request from him on Facebook. Back then, most people used Facebook; now, mostly, it's Instagram, and in the future, some other app may come. I was surprised that the person who left me before without any reason now took a step towards me. I accepted the request soon after seeing that. Initially, we chatted with each other so formally that we just had a discussion regarding our education during our first year of B.Tech. I was happy that he was talking to me. It took him two years to completely get to know me, and how much of a friendly connection I have with him. He used to say sorry for his rude behavior, avoiding me during our childhood, and thanking me for still treating him the same. At that time, I felt like whatever care, and affection we give to a person comes back to us, and that the concept of karma worked slowly but effectively. He is one of the people for whom I used to pray to God to always keep him happy. Surprisingly, he came to me with the same bond I have with him.

In our B.Tech third year, on my birthday, me, and my parents went to Vizag to offer prayers to Nookambika Devi, and I told him that I was going to the temple. After that, we stayed at our aunt's house that night, so he asked me, "Why can't we meet now?" With no second thought, he traveled miles away from his place, and I was waiting for him along with my two little cousins. I saw an auto going beside me; it was late evening, and I could still recognize that the person was my friend just by looking from the side view. Finally, we met each other, and we could see the happiness in our eyes. We talked a lot about how days passed, and now we became adults. We went to a nearby hangout, talked about our lives, and from then on, our friendship grew even more. That was the time we were meeting each other after 5 years; it was a good time to have a conversation with him. Going back home, I told Sunanda about him, saying that he is my childhood friend, and we have become good friends as of now, but it took years to form that bond. She was very happy that I had a bestie from my childhood. She talked to him at times over the phone, and soon they also became good friends. One of the things I loved about her is that she knew every friend of mine that she talked with, and got to know more about me; that was the best that she could give from her end. Once they met in Srinu's college as she went for an exam there. They felt good seeing each other, and these two people made fun of me, and got to know all things about me. At times, there were moments when Sunanda thought that I am mostly with Srinu. It might be true, but not completely, because both are my friends, and I have so much love to shower on them. He is the one to whom I gave my friendship voluntarily, and she is the one who offered her friendship to me as soon as I met her.

Every time Sunanda thinks of giving me the best, she always feels jealous if some other person tries to do so, but the thing is, no other person in my life has done that except her. She showered all her affection towards me in such a way that, in return, she just expected some love—very little because of human nature. I don't know how far, and how well I treated her, but she never let go of a single chance, which makes me happy. She loved my parents, my friends, and everyone who surrounded me to make me feel happy. We always have the best conversation while walking. In the afternoons, we went to the canteen to get some food or chips, and talked out of the box things when we really didn't know what to talk about, but we just had a conversation in such a way that it looked more like a debate. Whatever I say is completely the opposite of what she says, and vice versa. Our ultimate goal is the same, but we come through different paths. She always treated the gardeners, and other workers in the college with utmost respect; we went to them to wish them how they were, and she kept on asking about their well-being, and tried to make them feel solace with her happy words when they were too tired from cleaning the college.

One morning, we went to the canteen, and I saw a person preparing Dosa (the morning breakfast). I felt like I wanted to do that. All my friends laughed at my crazy thought, and this girl went inside, talked to the people, and took me there. She made my wish come true; I felt so happy preparing Dosa on such a big pan. It really made me feel so excited. I know that was a small, and crazy wish, but she took it seriously, and made my wish come true. That's how she made all my silly wishes come true, and she enjoyed it because I'm happy. She's such a sweet-hearted girl who finds happiness in other's smiles. A few can do that in one's life, and I can proudly say that she is the one in my life.

# 19

When we were in our final year of B.Tech, we all decided to be happier—no more fighting apart from everyday silly fights—we decided to make a lot of memories with each other, and have plenty of pictures. All we used to do was take pictures every day of those last moments. Later, we felt like we had to memorize them in our hearts, and not all can be captured with phones, on which Sravs sarcastically commented, "All those pictures will increase phone storage, for which you guys are cleverly saying moments should be remembered in hearts." We gave her a look as though we would all beat her together. You know every batch has this person who is calm, and innocent initially, and later that person makes the conversation too funny, whatever the situation may be. I think it's because they got bottled up until then, once they find someone with whom they are comfortable, they can't be calm anymore. We continued our talk, saying we have to live some moments completely, knowing that there should be nothing that disturbs our happiness, not even the phone. Sravs said, "Yeah" that yeah was so satirical again, we couldn't control this time, ended up teasing her, making her remember all those 1$^{st}$ year days when she was so calm, and innocent.

We tried to come out of all our fears, and anxiety that we had before. We solved our issues with our first-year batch, and again, we were together, there's no special need to highlight Sunanda's, and my bond; it's so precious. We all had our future plans, all these three girls mostly decided to stay at their home places, and find a job. Rather, I always wanted to go back to Hyderabad, and settle there. At times, Sunanda used to burst into tears that we were going to be together for that year itself. I consoled her, and said, "I'll be coming for you, and sure, I'll stay with you whenever I come back."

Days started moving quickly; actually, they're running. I know it was just a feeling, but I couldn't resist that. We enjoyed, and lived every single moment, preparing for campus interviews, aptitude, and reasoning, in which Sunanda gave her best knowledge to me. She is a quick learner; just by seeing, she can understand mostly, but she only pays attention when we are nearing our exams. During cultural activities, and other events in college, she used to be an anchor, and I used to write scripts on Teacher's day to make our lecturers feel surprised, and happy. We performed in skits, when there was any sort of disturbance, she settled down everything very spontaneously, and it seems like it's a part of the skit. She even modified many dialogues, and gave extra essence to the performance. We had the best faculty, and whatever they taught us was so impressive, especially when some of them taught us life, and history, it made all the students be silent, and attentive towards the speaker.

During our final year, Sunanda became chubby all of a sudden because of thyroid, and slowly she lost weight. Later, she became bubbly when she gained perfect health. It was our final-year project. Our batch was divided into two groups under our lecturer's guidance. They were so supportive, and made us strong enough with their life lessons as well as career guidance. We ourselves prepared each, and every chapter as per their instructions. The synopsis of the project was to reduce power consumption, and prevent battery overheating on mobile devices using various techniques. After all, I am an electronics' student, right? I felt the need to include at least a basic overview of the project, or else people might think there was no mention of studies at all. It was so fun, and interesting that we completed the project a month earlier than the deadline.

We were done with our presentations, and pdfs that we had to submit for our project, and they were about to come for print. We were so happy that we had completed a project, and it was getting transformed into a book. For this, we all decided to go to Vizag, and make prints so that we could have time to enjoy, and spend some time there. After a great discussion saying yes, and no, our trip got set, and we started the next morning on the train. We were all so excited; that was the first time we went so long. We were playing, talking to each other, arguing for no reason, enjoying the weather, everything. We reached the place, and gave an order for the books.

We got to know that it takes 3 hours to print them. We decided to go to the beach, and before that, we had our lunch in a restaurant where I sat beside Sravs, which made Sunanda a bit angry that she already kept a place beside her for me. I realized this soon, and tried to go to her when she was angry at me. I tried to explain it to her, but whenever she gets angry, it's not that easy for her to let it go soon;

she takes a lot of time, and I felt like this beach visit wouldn't be so good as she was angry. We went to the beach after having lunch. Seeing the beach made my heart feel so happy that there's some energy, some connection that one can feel on visiting a beach, the beauty of nature, the waves coming to, and fro, the sounds that come when the sea roars, the sand at the shore, which gives a tickling to one's feet, and the waves that touch feet give a feel that we are going into the sea along with them.

All these little things add aesthetic beauty to the place. But all these were just not giving me completeness because she's not talking to me; she was not interested in taking photos with me but was taking selfies with some other friends. I was low, and sat alone at the shore, and wrote SMSB on the sand; it looked so good on it, and looking into the sea, my mind went on thinking about life: what will I be doing next, and how could the future be after a year? There were swings in my thoughts. I smiled inside because I was thinking too much, and suddenly she came, and touched my hand.

Soon I came to the reality. She said, "Let's fight some other day, as we can't get a day like this, so let's make this moment as memorable as possible." I chuckled, and we started running here, and there, holding each other's hands. We got so wet that we went into the water, and enjoyed that moment so heartfully, and we girls felt like we were the most deserving candidates to have all the happiness in this world. When you live with your friends, no other moment can be as good as it is with them. A moment ago, I lost myself just because she was angry at me, and I couldn't see the true beauty of that place. Soon, she talked to me my words changed, my happiness rose, and it was the best moment. Nature grew itself more, and more beautiful. That's how the bond creates an impact on your surroundings when you are with your dear ones. As we had a habit of doing TikToks a lot, we decided to take one video where we girls were sitting at the shore facing the sea. From behind, we were having a song, putting each other's hands on our shoulders from the 1st person to the 4th person, we were swinging from right to left. Even when the video was recording, we were talking about something. It was one of the most memorable videos we ever had together as SMSB.

There were mangoes near the seashore. Sunanda loves them, only the unripe ones, so we bought mango slices, and ate them. We captured some beautiful views, and sat together, just looking at the beach we lost ourselves. Then I felt like asking Srinu to come over there. I called him, as he was nearby. He came, and met me. I was so happy to see him again after a long time. I was talking to him as soon as Sunanda saw him, she dragged him to the beach. As of then, they were also good friends, we captured those moments, and shared our happiness among each other. It was evening when we collected our books, and got on the bus after giving a send-off to Srinu. We were so tired that we couldn't even talk. We slept in the bus as soon as it started moving. As there was a speed breaker, I woke up, and saw her innocent face. Sunanda was sleeping. Looking into her face, I prayed to God that she should get all the happiness in this world even when I'm not with her. She should be strong enough, and be blessed with a healthy life. I started thinking about all our four years of memories; they were flashing in front of me one after the other. Fights, fun, crying, togetherness, laughing madly at each other, standing next to each other when in trouble, and no trouble. I was a bit emotional thinking what will I do when she's not around me. Then there was a brake as we reached our place, and there was a break on my thoughts too.

# 20

## The Final Moments

We were getting close to our final year's final semester. B.Tech life was at its last days, and moments. For a while, we felt so happy that we were going to get our bachelor's degree, and immediately the latter thought was that we were going to miss each other—those beautiful days, those wonderful moments, funny behavior, mischievous things, fights, happiness, what not everything. This thought made us pale, but the remembrance of the past brought a smile on our faces. Days started heading like flash light again, we went to watch a movie to add one more memory to our diaries. We enjoyed the good food after that, and just had a simple conversation about nothing but something. We prepared for our exams well, for the very last time, for the very last exams of B.Tech life. We had conference calls, and explained the subjects to each other, just like before as we were given preparation holidays. I have Sunanda's call recording in which she explained the topics of the next day's exam.

Before exams, Sunanda asked me, "Let's go to a place where we'd be strangers to the world, and just relax." I replied, "Come home tomorrow; I'll take you to a place the way you expect." She got excited, and I was thinking of the place— where should we go, and would she like it or not? The next day, I was waiting at the bus stop to receive her. Seeing me, she ran fast towards me, and asked, "So now, where are we going?" With bright teeth, and twinkling eyes. I smiled, looking at her, took her to a village nearby. Narayanapuram, is the village name. That was where my mom, and dad took me and my brother when we shifted from Hyderabad. I felt excited, and admired its beauty, so she too would love the place. It is what I thought, and planned to take her there. We traveled through the farms for some time, and she asked me where we were going throughout the journey, and I kept it a short, and sweet surprise for her. Once we reached the village, I told her, "We are going to a temple that is very special; it has more than hundreds of years of history. It is said that the temple was built by gods, and goddesses. Every night, they used to come to the Earth, and construct the temple. In the morning, the place looked normal, but during the night, the temple appeared, and would be under construction, the process continued. In the early hours, one day a washer man was passing the place, saw the temple being constructed by the gods, and goddesses. He ran away from the place, and called all his fellow people to see the wonder that took place. After he said the news, he died over there, the temple was left unconstructed, and gods disappeared from the place." As I narrated, we reached the temple. At the entrance, there will be a stone, and it is believed that the washer man became a stone once he died. She looked at the stone in surprise, and asked me, "How did you know all this?" I just shrugged, and said, "My dad told me." We entered the temple, had the darshan of Lord Shiva, and offered our prayers. The temple is completely constructed with stones, and it has some lipi written on each stone of the entire construction. The left side of the temple has a Lord Ganesh statue, and the right side has a Parvathi Devi idol. The entire temple has a peaceful atmosphere; she loved the place, and it was a cool morning as the Sun felt not to disturb our happiness by his heat, he hid behind the clouds. I thanked him in my heart. We ate the prasadam offered to us in the temple as we felt hungry at that time, we ate it happily, and sat there for some time while discussing all our happiest moments, and later inhaled the peace of that place. She then said, “I loved this place, and it’s really a great place to visit, so I think this is the place we came for. Shall we go now?” I said, “No, not now; still, we are left to see the beauty of this place.” She happily stood up, and said, “Let’s move, and explore the leftover beauty of this place.” By eating the prasadam, I walked along with her. Walking for less than a mile, we heard the roaring of water. She exclaimed, “Is it a river?" I simply nodded. We climbed some rocks over there, taking ups, and downs, and finally we reached a running river. She stood calm. I explained, “The river is named Suvarnamukhi, and it is one of the best places that I have seen so far.” She reached the river, touched the water, and ran them across her fingers from one hand to the other. She moved forward to let the water touch her legs up to her ankles. I stood, and watched, letting her enjoy herself in her own way. She looked deep inside the water, taking all the positive vibes through it, and looked at me. I walked towards her, and we sprinkled water on each other. While walking here and there at the shore of the river, the sand crystals ran over our legs; they tickled our feet, yet it didn't bother us much. We inhaled the fresh air, the sprinkles of water that touched our faces often added more pleasantness for us. We sat there for a while talked nothing, we were just so silent, and that silence is filled with our happiness. We looked at each other holding our hands, we started walking again. We didn't capture any pictures; we just wanted the moment to stick in our lives, and to remind us of every second of happiness when we close our eyes, and remember that day. We then left the place, and reached our home. My mom welcomed her with a big, and tight hug, Sunanda enthusiastically narrated every place she saw. After a long discussion, we ate enough, and again engaged in our talk, and crazy stuff. She left the place early in the evening, as she had to travel for more than an hour. The day was well spent, and I felt happy giving her what she wanted.

Our exams were in April, and during one exam, we had Sunanda's birthday. I thought of doing this, and that, what not? everything. I day dreamed of celebrating her birthday just like every year. I shouldn't say this, but somehow, I couldn't even give her anything. It made me feel shy that I couldn't stand in front of her, the girl whom I love the most, the girl who cares for me a lot, the girl who celebrated my birthday so grandly that in return, I did nothing for her. A day before, she told me that she was not interested in all those things because of some reasons. Hearing that, I didn't want to put her in more pain by doing all that stuff again, so I just wished her, and recorded an audio of my voice with a slideshow of her photos. She came to college looking so dull. I couldn't do anything but simply stand by her side, I was there. I really didn't like not celebrating, and seeing her sad, but I'll be bounded by her words. We completed exam, and I asked her if we could celebrate. She didn't say a word but gestured which showed her denial. I wished her again, hugged her, and left the place. A day before, Sravs called me, and said we should celebrate the day, but I really thought it wouldn't work out. This was the greatest pain, and embarrassment I felt for not celebrating her day. But Sravs, on the other side, along with some other friends somehow convinced her, and made her day by cutting cake, and doing celebrations. I felt so happy—at least she made her day—I felt a bit sorry for her for not being a part in her happiness. In the evening, I talked to Sunanda. We had some conversation, yet that guilt was killing me inside. She was also a bit upset that I was not there by that time, which made her happiness incomplete along with few other reasons.

We had more than 10-days gap after that exam, so I thought of surprising Sunanda, and ordered a watch, and that frame, which we all have. I collected both of them. Sravs, and I went to her home, and gave her a surprise. As usual, Mouni didn't come there; every time she had the habit of missing every occasion, as usual she even missed then. That was the day we three had ultimate happiness. I don't know what gave us that happiness, but we had it. I finally succeeded in giving Sunanda a day full of happiness with no regrets post her birthday. We had lunch, made TikToks along with our sister, had some family time with her parents, and in the evening, she took me, and Sravs to the complex on her scooty. We really enjoyed that moment. She called me after reaching home, and said that she was happy, which brought a smile on my face.

Finally, it was the last exam in the other college. We wrote the exam quickly, and came out. All four of us sat together in a row. We knew we were emotional that we were unable to utter a word at that time. Within a short time, we realized that we had to make that moment happy, and laughed at each other while cracking jokes, we went to the canteen, had parotta, ate enough, and came out. While walking, we remembered every second of those valuable four years by crying inside, and smiling outside. After some time, Mouni left the place saying she had to go home even though we requested her to stay, angerness she would show so easily but she won't show love often. Sravs, Sunanda, and I were sitting at a place, and thought of one final TikTok. The video is for 10 seconds, but it took an hour because we were laughing, and at some point, something went wrong in the video, background, etc. Later, Sravs was talking to some other friends, but me, and Sunanda couldn't be apart from each other, as we knew after that it would take time for our next meeting.

Unexpectedly, the last day we were wearing the same type of dress with the same color combination, which made us feel happy. Both of us wore simple orange colored tops. We walked towards the see-saw, sat on the opposite side, and started swinging. She got scared, and cried like a child. I laughed at her being unable to control the expressions she made while crying like a kid. Later, we went to a nearby place that we had never seen. There was a guest house that looked so scary, I recorded a video in which we shared our experiences regarding that place. It looked like a haunted house. We moved forward, holding each other's hands, talking about the place, and suddenly we saw so mango trees nearby. When we reached there, there were no mangoes, we were disappointed a bit and were about to leave that place, soon she saw plenty of mangoes on a tree; we plucked two mangoes, and left the place. It was like a treasure hunt. In return, we found our treasure in the form of mangoes. We then went to the top floor of the college, viewed the aerial view, which was very pleasant with greenery all around us, and captured some pictures. Later we both spent time walking here, and there, and having soft drinks. I gave her chocolates, she felt happy seeing them. It was late evening, and we had to leave the place. We couldn't bear the feeling of getting apart, but we had to, as it was late, and no one was there apart from some of our friends. We wrote SMSB for one last time together on the road with water. I hugged Sravs, and we walked straight down the road, and waited for the auto, as I had to go in the opposite direction than the rest of the people, I hugged Sunanda for the last time, which made us feel like we were not apart anymore. Tears rolled down her eyes. I made her laugh with pain inside. She scolded me, and we laughed at each other, holding each other's hands. There, we saw an auto coming close to us. I closed my eyes, and prayed for the auto to be full, and so it was. We felt happy looking at each other, I guess she too had prayed the same, as I could sense that through her hands, which were holding mine. But it lasted no longer; there came another auto that I had to get in. I could feel her hand holding me tight, which shows her pain in that touch of getting apart. I got in, and still my hand was within hers, and then the auto started moving, we couldn't leave each other, but we had to. That time, I just saw our hands holding together, and how they were slowly getting distant. The space between our hands was bridged by our emotions, and the bond we have. I saw her smiling face hiding pain inside, so I thought of getting down, and catching up with another auto later, but I couldn't because it makes us feel even more emotional. I smiled, and waved back. There were many of my friends beside her waving back to me, but my eyes were only on her. I looked at her until my eyes could see; she was far beyond my eyesight, and then there was only an empty road further. I went into thoughts, thinking of the time when we will meet again. Is it as usual tomorrow in the same class? No. Is it after a week, just like after holidays? No. So when, I don't know, but I got my answer "Soon." Soon I will see her, which made me feel happy, and then there was a brake. I reached my home, and as usual, it was a break for my thoughts too.

I'm lucky enough to see her again soon within a month, but it was quite an unexpected situation that she went for her cousin's marriage where she fell down, and got her leg fractured. She was taken to the hospital, and was supposed to take one month of bed rest, but she had an exam that she was supposed to write in another college. When she told me about her leg fracture, I said, "No worries, you come to college along with your father; I'll take care of you" to which she replied "Okay." On May 25, 2019, she had the exam, and came to college along with her father. I teased her for a while, then took her in, holding her very carefully. She was not able to walk, and needed a person to support her. I felt bad seeing her that way, slowly took her to the exam room and made her sit at the allotted place to write the exam. I put her leg on another bench just to give her support so that she won't have that much pain, and can write her exam comfortably. I waited outside till she finished her exam. After writing the exam she was walking towards me, seeing her, I ran, and took her into my hands. At one point, I felt that if I had enough strength to hold her in my arms, I wouldn't let her walk; instead, I would lift, and carry her. We talked for a while, later her father came back to take her home. I told her to take care of herself, she was going far from me on the bike, which made me remember her pain on that day when I was going away from her in the auto. That feeling is very bad to experience, yet the thought of seeing her again made me feel better, and I went home.

# 21

It was not more than a month since I left my hometown, I started thinking about my career because my ultimate goal was to get settled, stand by my parents, and other family members. A day started in Hyderabad at my grandparent's home, which is the most comfortable, and the happiest place for me. I was planning regarding my career, what are the coaching's that I was supposed to take, or any direct job. I started applying for jobs through different sites, trying to learn new things. Finally, I joined in a coaching institute at Ameerpet-Maitrivanam, which is famous for its coaching centers. We can see thousands of students on those streets to learn new things, and when I was there, I realized how many students are struggling for their jobs to have a good career with great work.

In the beginning, I was frightened by the extent of unemployment in that place. If that specific area had so many students, what about the city, states, and countries? This thought sent a shiver through my heart. My parents, and friends provided me with enough strength. I used to travel early mornings on crowded buses, often standing at the entrance step, making it seem like I might fall. Spending the entire day in the institute, learning new things, I returned late evenings after practicing in labs. If I had some time, I talked to Sunanda, who always reassured me that everything would be set right soon, boosting my concentration. The first time I attended an interview at an MNC, I still remember I reached my destination by taking a bus, then an auto, and walking a few miles to save money. I didn't get selected in my first interview; I knew I lacked confidence, often trembling while answering or pausing during speech. Going to coaching, and attending interviews became my daily routine. I was so focused on my career that I never had a second thought. I rarely spoke to Sunanda, making her feel alone, but she understood me. Whenever I called her, the only question she had was, "When are you coming to me?" I used to say soon; she was disappointed, yet somehow, we managed by reminiscing about our college days. We recalled that one day near exams, we celebrated Holi by smearing colors on each other. It was the first time we played Holi together, and wrote our signatures on uniforms, a tradition most graduates follow during their last year in college. We had many pictures together. This conversation bridged the distance, and we smiled wholeheartedly.

Gradually, I became entirely focused on setting my career path, and we seldom talked. It was during this time that she was facing some health issues, which I wasn't aware of as I was immersed in building my career. Despite her health concerns, she never complained. When we did talk, she mostly encouraged me to forge a good path. There were moments when I felt discouraged about not getting hired, which made me feel low. However, I managed to pull myself together, and prepared afresh for the next competitive day.

I don't know how much we enjoyed college, but at that time, I felt miles away from that word. In everyone's life, there comes a crucial phase when one focuses only on their career to build a life that they have dreamt of until then. It prompts you to contemplate the good, and bad, the profits, and losses, and the multitude of skills to be acquired. Most importantly, it makes you question how determined you are for tomorrow, even if you face setbacks today.

In the beginning, we may feel like we can't do anything, but there should be self-motivation. If we can't motivate ourselves, then we should seek help from others or should try to analyze things by observing. Often, when we look around with an open mind, the solution lies in nature itself. However, it becomes apparent when we are strong enough.

# 22

Time was moving in its routine, but I felt like I was running out of days. I improved my skills, but still at one point, I used to get rejected. There were times I was almost done but couldn't get placed, which gave me a great kick. I used to get mood swings. At times I'd be concentrating more, and at other times nothing. I thought of going back to my mom, and staying with her so I could also gather with my friends. Soon I realized my responsibilities, and started practicing.

I only had SMSB contact; we had video calls rarely, and my friend Srinu, who always helped me learn. Day by day, the graph fell so drastically that I didn't talk to them from days to weeks, and weeks to a month. I still remember how this affected Sunanda; she had no one to share her feelings with yet somehow managed, and even when we talked to each other, she still asked me about how it was going, and never complained that I wasn't talking to her. I know she used to feel bad, and alone inside, which she couldn't tell anyone. At times, I used to send her some pictures of her diary so that she could stay strong after seeing them. While traveling, I used to think of those beautiful college days, and text her. Sunanda used to bring amchur, which is her favorite time pass eating, and I really didn't like it. She used to eat that daily in packets, and share it with some other friends. Then one day she gave it to me as I thought of having something. I ate it, and from then onwards I started liking it, and she used to bring those packets more. Afternoon lunch time jokes, making fun of each other, doing all crazy stuff, and acting like innocent, canteen memories, walking ahead the corridor, in the ground, traveling, bunking, movies, gossips—whatever, each, and every moment appeared like a flash with a great delight from the bottom of my heart. One day, I remember that we two were the only people who went to college during the end of the semester, and unexpectedly wore the same type of dress in a red, and black color combination. It was the day when we talked throughout, took hundreds of pictures, laughed seeing each other, and had a great time together. A person can forget all his worries, and pain when he is with the best person; again, the best is not in the sense of completeness. It's the value that you give to the other person by seeing them from previous days to years, and treating them as your own. I can strongly say that we have that connection together. As of today, we both don't know each other's favorite color, movie, etc., but we both do know how we're going to handle a situation together.

# 23

After a continuous effort, I finally got placed in one of the top-most MNCs, I was extremely happy that I was literally waiting for a chance to enter MNC. It took almost 3 days for interviews, HR rounds, and document submission. I told my parents, and family members they were so happy for that, and I told the same to Sunanda, and other friends. Everyone was so happy, and wished me a successful career. I still remember that evening when I was going back home, all the efforts, and rejections played in front of my eyes.

A day before entering the company, there were some formalities to be completed, and I didn't even have a laptop. It was Srinu who helped me come out of the trouble, and supported me till midnight in submitting all documents, and other formalities. Entering the company was half of my effort, and the other support, and help to submit documents was completely from him. This fellow was a job holder even before graduating from B.Tech. He worked for a German-based company as a full-stack developer, and has abundant knowledge in coding, I'm the girl who didn't even know how to write the "Hello World" program. He helped me during college to get to know the loopholes of coding, and how a program runs. I can say that I have one male bestie who will always be my support.

The first day I entered the company, it was like, wow. The building was very large, as it was the main building of the company. I was the only girl who reached the office so early that it was still 7 a.m. in the morning, as we were supposed to be there by 8 a.m. sharp. Yeah, I know I reached beforehand, but what should I do? It was my grandpa who told me to reach early because of traffic in Hyderabad, and to be punctual from day one.

I was looking at the office premises, which had such a professional entry. At a distance from the reception, people were sitting straight in a dignified posture. I sat on the sofa, which was very smooth, the kid in me woke up saying jump on it. I ignored the thought, and started behaving very professional, making my body language comfortable to avoid nervousness. I clicked some pictures where we are allowed to click, as in that place inside, we were prohibited from taking snaps in restricted areas but could have them at some places, I sent them to Sunanda.

After more than an hour, the new joiners started coming one after the other. We all sat together with an employee who collected all our documents, and the first day was done engaging in legal formalities. It was a great day for which I had been waiting for ages, and my imagination manifested that day. I was living the day for which I had been struggling, and therefore, I was satisfied. Soon we shifted to our client's company, where we were supposed to work. I tell you this was the building, seeing which I stood astonished.

The entrance seemed just normal, and the way we entered, there was a large place that was set for a garden area with beautiful plants, and trees around, different types of roses with a good fragrance welcoming in. The doors for entrance were automatically sensored. A few meters away, there was a reception that was very different, and uniquely structured. Looking up, there was a big chandelier glimpsing gold-colored. It was so big, which changed the whole entrance's beauty, and the straight wall was adorned with greenery and had a few flower pots hanging from it. We sat on the sofa, waiting for our names to be called. After an hour or so, we were allowed in. There, we had a cafeteria. We went in, and it was such a large, and a beautiful hangout where there were different types of fruits, salads, breakfast, juices, milk, cornflakes, and what not. All the Indian, and Western breakfasts were available around. We ate enough, and went into the conference room, seeing every time how large the rooms were, our eyes got habituated slowly, and we went in, there was clear guidance on dos, and don'ts given by the security department.

We were later given our ID cards. Seeing that, and holding it in my hands, I got goosebumps, and finally, I'm starting my professional career. The thought boosted me more. Seeing myself as so professional, I was happy, and shared those moments with Sunanda, who was very happy listening to all that. Within a week, we got our cabs rostered, and we were set for training. The very first day I boarded the cab was really an awesome memory in my life. I got ready for the office thinking the way I used to get ready for school, and college: wearing the ID. I don't know why, but I love wearing the ID card; it gives me enough happiness.

Even in my childhood, I always used to wear IDs, on the other hand Sunanda never had a habit of doing that. During viva, and exams, we forced her to put on the ID. I still have my school, and college IDs, which brings some nostalgic feeling. I got a call from my cab driver that he was waiting. My grandpa, and I went down, and I boarded the cab. Seeing me boarding the cab, I could see happiness in his eyes, and finally, I'm here, fulfilling their wishes.

The cab moved on. I was recollecting everything—my past, and present, how things changed, and I'm blessed. While moving into Hi-Tech city, the IT hub, I remembered how I used to walk on the roads, searching for a job so determinedly, traveled to the place mostly on foot to save money for some other day. I never went to a restaurant or bought something to eat just to save money. As of today, I'm traveling in a car provided by the company. How things changed in a span of months, and how I used to travel to school, and college, how I walked alone with disappointment, and hope, that brought a smile on my face.

Seeing that, finally, I felt inside that I am set. Never ever think of giving up. I know that once people become successful, they come up with these kinds of statements. Even I used to think that way, but once we build the path, the journey gives us the realization of how life tests us. While recollecting fun, and laughing in college, soon there was a brake on the cab, and on my thoughts too.

# 24

Since the day I joined the company, I had been completely surrounded by work. It started early in the mornings, and I used to come home late in the evenings. I talked to my family, and Sunanda while I was having lunch or a small break, and days used to be so busy. When I got stuck in my work life, soon I realized I was getting far from relations; I only knew that these people would understand me, and so they are. When I had my week offs, I used to talk for hours with my family, and friends. I know that Sunanda was unable to share each, and every feeling with me. But we know that when we meet again, it will be great, and beautiful, full of endless delight, and we will cry with joy.

While going to the office, I saw a hospital, and remembered a funny incident we had. One day, Sunanda was feeling sick, we asked her to get some rest, and recover. Instead, she came to college, so Mouni, and I took her to the hospital, for which she refused throughout the way. We teased her. A girl who can talk in front of thousands of people in an auditorium is afraid of a single doctor. It hurt her ego, so she said, "No, I'm not afraid of anyone; let's go." We laughed looking at her, went in, and took an appointment.

We were at the entrance of the consulting room when this girl suddenly started crying, we thought her pain was heavy. She said, "It's not the pain; it's because of the injection that the doctor gives, that's what I'm afraid of." In the meantime, the doctor saw all this, and asked us to come in, and inquire, "Which class are you studying in?" She replied, "B.Tech final year", and the doctor bursted into laughter. "Being almost a graduate, you are afraid of injections; I thought you are still in your school." She said, "Don't worry, I'm not giving you any injections; instead, take some tablets that I prescribe, and if you again say you are afraid of this too, I'll give you an injection." Sunanda grabbed the prescription quickly. We came out, looked at her face, and laughed like anything. She is such a brave girl, yet she is afraid of injections, and cockroaches; once she saw a cockroach in one of the washrooms, she never used it again. There are some funny moments that I remember, and feel happy when I am not with her.

# 25

Within a few days it was my birthday, and all my family, and friends wished me, as usually Sunanda wished me in the morning, I don't know why but that was the time I felt so lonely, I have a job, and my family surrounding me but that enjoyment, and fun was lost just because she was not beside me. She put a lot of status for me yet I didn't receive a single status on WhatsApp. There was some technical glitch so she sent me all the screenshots of her status, and two videos which she edited with our photos. Still, I missed her presence. We talked for a while in the evening, and I felt solace in her words. After a few days, it was the day of my first salary, and I still remember that day when I received it. I was returning home in the evening after work, a notification popped up on my phone. I was so happy that I received my first pay. I withdrew money from a nearby ATM, and gave it to my grandfather, he returned it to me saying "Keep it with you", and I again handed the money to him saying, "Keep them with you, grandpa," and took his blessings. I was glad that a day came in my life that I was giving something to my family in return. I shared my happiness with Sunanda, and the day ended with utmost satisfaction.

It was a month since I joined the company. There was a pandemic that the world suffered. It started in China in December 2019, and made the whole world know how dreadful it was. The virus was named Corona-Covid19. The virus traveled the whole world, and so it was in India by March 2020. Previously, the year 2020 was expected to be the most economically developed year, but it was the year which fell drastically down not only in the economy but also affected millions of people with a huge loss worldwide. Soon, the virus grew more, and more, most of the people lost their dear ones, there was no vaccine for it by that time, and the central government decided to start a lockdown in India, it was already implemented in other countries as well. In our office, we had an announcement that they were closing down the company for some days as the pandemic is getting severe. From that day we had holidays. It had just been a month since I joined the company, and my friends made fun of this issue because you achieved something, the whole world got shut down, and they teased me. I started preparing more, and more crafts, as throughout the whole day everyone was free. I used to utilize most of the time in crafts, and talking to my friends in the evenings, having fun with my brother, preparing home-made food etc. People used to go to market once in a week, in the evenings, and the areas which had a higher number of Corona positive cases were under the containment zone. Scientists and doctors were trying their best, that was the time everyone got to know the sacrifice made by the covid front-line warriors, who risked their lives to save others, it was the virus which separated people from their beloved ones. There was a lockdown for days, and there was no single human on the roads. With this at some places wild animals used to come on roads just to know where the human beings went.

Sunanda's birthday was getting near in April, and I thought of sending her a gift as I was employed by that time. The virus was so dreadful that there were not even deliveries available at that time. I asked Sravs to buy a gift, and surprise her but there was a complete, and strict lockdown in their area because of red alert, and was under containment zone so people were not going to each other's home. There was some fight happening between me, and Sunanda. We were not talking to each other on some issues, but somehow, we soon talked with a bit of affection outside, and as usual our inner feeling was to meet, and talk to each other. It was her birthday. I greeted her in the night through SMS because I missed her next to me, and the next morning I called her, and talked to her. I was literally disappointed that even having money I was unable to send her a gift. I recollected all our four years of journey together. I smiled, and made myself stronger. I hoped I will be with her next year, and that thought made me happy, and active again.

# 26

Seeing our photos, and thinking of our memories, one day she called me, and talked so happily, she sent hundreds of emojis just to bring a smile on my face, and of course I was happy too. The immediate day she called me, and told me all her loneliness, how she was feeling by that time, and how much she missed me, it hit me like a bow shot from my back. We realized how much we missed each other.

As usual, we had that fun conversation, some tragic talks, and which again were hit back by satirical jokes, I was happy that finally we were back to each other. I remember that day I was cleaning our home. Though I was busy mopping the floor, I managed myself carrying a mop in one hand, mobile in the other, and talked to her as it had been many days we were talking to each other wholeheartedly. Some conversations need not be very fairy nor very dramatical just they need to be kept on so that everything becomes normal, and even more satisfying, and again, from that day we talked for more time, she suddenly used to become alone, and I kept her active again, after which she used to gain herself back. I don't know why but whenever she speaks to me, she feels very relaxed. I love that happiness in her, and of course why not, she is my magic to regain myself too.

Days passed very rapidly. When we talk, we used to discuss our four years of journey, within no time it was Mouni who got engaged, and was ready to get married, we felt so happy that she was the very first girl in our batch to get married soon, and the thought of going to hometown so that we can meet each other, and attend her marriage made me feel very excited and the thought of seeing Sunanda made me more excited. But fate was quite different. There was no transport available by that time, and we were unable to do anything. It was about the end of summer, and her marriage date got fixed, we managed to order some silver item from local shops, and made it reach to her on the wedding day, of course she was angry upon us that none of us have gone there. Yet, we had a great conversation through video call which lasted for more than an hour even though it was her wedding. We all were so happy that she was the first girl who was getting married among SMSB, and, deep inside we all knew we missed each other. Though she was happy to see the gift that we sent her, she still missed us, and we too missed her on one of the important days when we were supposed to be together. We enjoyed those cute moments virtually through video call on her wedding day, and they were captured in our hearts.

After 2-3 days, one day Sunanda said her health was getting worse day by day, and she was unable to manage herself, this made me feel worried yet she strengthened me saying, “I'll be okay, you don't worry about me.” The other day, she said, “You'll never come to me no matter what happens to me.” I don't know what stopped me, every time I thought of going, I was unable to get started. After coming from my hometown, a year had passed since I met her, and this thought gave pain to such an extent that tears rolled out of my eyes. She used to send some videos, and some of our photos to cheer up herself as well as me, she is the one who scolded me for not coming to her, and she is the one who stood by my side when she understood my situation without my single word of explanation, and to this girl I used to say, “You can never understand me or anyone.” I don't know how much it hurt her but her support made me realize she was the one who understood me, I realized within myself. One fine day, she sent me a message saying let's take a mobile back cover with our picture on it. This was the thought we had during our college days but by that time we didn't have those big phones. I replied, "Okay, but by next month I'm planning to have a new mobile. Once I get it, we can print it on our phones." We were so happy that after a long year of waiting we were going to have our mobile back covers with our photos on them.

# 27

The happiest conversations took place for most of the days; everything was healing; we were just missing physical presence, but our souls were interconnected. When I think of her, the next moment there will be a call or text from her, and vice versa.

In June, our sister's birthday was getting near after Mouni's marriage, so she sent me some pictures, and asked me to choose the present, and I selected a bracelet; we ordered that. It was the year she celebrated our sister's birthday so grand that she never did it before. Later, in the same month, it was Sunanda's mother's birthday. As all were in that month itself, one after the other, we were happy, and joyous. Whatever she buys or presents to someone, she always has a discussion with me before. Can we choose this or not? Though she's an expert in a good selection. We ordered a beautiful pair of bangles for aunty, but unfortunately, they were replaced with earrings somehow, and we ended up receiving an unexpected order. We were disappointed with that last-minute shock, but she managed to present another gift to aunty. She sent me every picture of the celebration, and how they enjoyed the day, seeing my Sona (the nickname I gave her long ago) happy, I was at cloud nine. Her complete happiness every time gives me immense pleasure.

After a very strict lockdown, our office got started again, and we were again busy with work life. One morning, she called me, when I was busy helping my grandma with work. She argued with me to talk to her, and I felt happy that after a very long gap, she asked me that way. It mostly happened during our college days; if one of us was working on something, the other would argue to listen to all the things that happened that day. I managed my work, and talked to her. That was the day she talked to me wholeheartedly since we graduated college. I can feel that day as of today also. She complained about my faults, and my ignorance during our reunion fight. I laughed at her, and complained back the same, but every time she complains, I feel she is much more honest than me in our bond, and better at caring compared to me. When she speaks, I can't complain because everything seems so perfect in her statements, and I'll be just quiet, and attentive to what she is saying. We had a beautiful conversation that day, and all our misunderstandings faded away with her magical words. I recorded her voice, which I listen to at times when I miss her.

# 28

A day started as an indication of misery, never expected even in dreams but so it happened. That morning she texted me saying her health was not at all good. Last night in the middle of sleep, when she tried to lift her hand, she failed and it hurt her so much. I was worried, soon I called her, she didn't pick up my call, and texted back. "No worries, now I'm fine." She asked me not to tell anyone as everyone shows sympathy, we had a chat for a while after she healed, and we also cracked some jokes on each other. The next night she had the same pain, and told her mom, and dad, they took her to the hospital. Those days were having a very strict lockdown because of covid cases no one was allowed to go out, as her father is a journalist, and her mom an ANM in hospital, they managed to get her treated in the hospital.

There everyone was so busy, and rushed here, and there due to a lot of emergencies. She was getting treated under the guidance of a doctor, a nurse came, and set IV set to her hand with which she had unbearable pain, and started crying, soon the doctor arrived, and scolded the nurse to remove IV set which was completely not necessary for her condition, and before that the nurse gave an injection to her. After treatment they reached home, she called me, and explained everything even in that pain. During the night she again got a pain in her back for which her mother told it's because of the injection, no worries everything will be alright by the next morning which was actually not.

A few days passed, one day she felt sore, and swelling on her back where she had an injection. She used to put ice on that area for temporary relief. She called me, and talked to me to get rid of that pain. We used to have some other usual conversation, and fun talk as we couldn't talk about her health every time which would make her feel low, we changed to different topics like JAM (Just A Minute) sessions in college, and since she couldn't talk much, we avoided debates which we usually had in college. I used to talk to her while going to the office, and then coming back home at times, and later in the evenings, we used to text each other.

Distance was the biggest mistake in our lives consciously or because of destiny I don't know but there were times, I need to be with her to support her. To my sin, I couldn't. We connected only via phones, and video calls. When we keep on talking, and sharing our feelings, that hundreds of kilometres distance just fades away with the thought "SOUL." We were just hundreds of kilometers away, no other parameters stopped us connecting, and exchanging our feelings, and at that time, I felt like showing my gratitude towards technology just because of source, channel, and destination as main parameters, we hear each other which seems very unusual but actually it works. I remember she used to say these words.

# 29

Slowly her condition was getting worse day by day, that part where she got injection, got completely swollen. She had an operation for that after getting an appointment with the doctor which was very difficult because of covid scenario. Her parents, and she visited the hospital daily just to get an appointment, though she had no strength she managed herself to go to the hospital. To our bane, one of the staffs was tested positive for coronavirus which led to closing down the hospital for few days, and there was no other hospital for operations than that. She stopped eating much, and couldn't bear pain any longer. Before getting treated, every day we used to talk to each other. I don't know how far it healed her but it gave a temporary relief, and put a smile on her face. I was somewhat happy that I was making her smile in that condition but the pain gradually depressed her physically, and mentally. At times, she used to laugh just to make her surroundings feel comfortable, and when she couldn't bear the pain she used to burst into tears, hearing her scream made my heart feel very bad. Her father was depressed, and thought he was the reason for not getting her treated properly at the time when she had to get treated. But the fact was some other thing, to make him feel happy, and normal even in that condition she mentally prepared herself, and used to be quite normal which is very painful in real life.

Those days were very hard for her to pass even a single second, she cried when no one watched her. She used to say what was my biggest mistake, that I'm suffering this much pain. I don't know how to heal her but I only listened to her, and after all her sayings the only thing I said, "You are getting well soon, and we'll be happy just like before." After a long wait later, they got an appointment from the doctor, and she had an operation successfully. I was happy that soon she would be normal, and things will be fine. That evening she gained conscious, and came back home, called me, and said she's fine, and hearing her voice with a bit of a comfortable tone soothed me.

Within no days they realized that the cut was very deep, it started bleeding, house surgeons used to come home, and dress her daily so as not to get infected. To dress her up, the bandage should be removed, and clean the wound with some medical stuff, while doing so I used to call her, and tried to divert but of no use, the pain was so severe she screamed, hearing her pain, and the thought of distance literally killed me inside, her anguish was that loud that all their neighbors surrounded the house, and got to know how much pain she was suffering from. After an hour or two she slowly gained herself, and I know how hard it's for her to gain back strength. Even in that condition to cherish me she called back, and talked so normal, and later prayed that no one should suffer the pain that she had. She used to tell me how the neighbors surrounded her home, and made her smile to set things normal, and assured that she would be hale, and healthy again. She used to say come for me at least once, and later she said I know you won't come whatever happens to me, these words made me speechless, and I accepted because it was completely my inconvenience. Every time I planned to go home some obstacles stopped me. When she realized my position, she again made me feel comfortable. I don't know whether to be happy because of her spirit or to cry because I was not standing beside her in that tough situation. Day by day the bleeding was heavy, she had a loss in her haemoglobin levels. Meanwhile, the pain spread up to her legs that she neither stood properly nor sit or sleep. She used to sleep only turning to one side, and can't turn to the other side as the pain was severe, imagining her pain made me feel very heavy but she was the one who suffered alone, and how she managed herself was really her inner strength completely.

# 30

I used to go to the office, and come back home as a daily routine, subconsciously I used to think of her how she was, and when are things going back to normal. One day, when I was having a chat with her, she said, “Everyone is showing pity on me, I’m unable to take this extra burden.” I said, “Why do you think that? Just see how people love you, and how concerned they are” to which she replied, “Pain is completely mine, no one can take this, and I have to suffer this all alone but this sympathy is making me feel nervous.” I couldn’t say anything even if I wanted to argue like in college days. For every single statement of mine she had a counter statement. It’s not because she wanted to argue, it’s because of her pain she talked so. To get back into those B.Tech days, if possible, would be the best days of our lives I thought to myself so that I can stick with her. She reminded me with one of our memories when we were having a conversation. One afternoon in college, after lunch we went upstairs, and sat there to chill out. For some reason Mouni didn’t come to college that day, Sunanda bought a cone (Mehendi) with her, and said she would put mehendi on my hands. I said "No, not now", and yes, she finally took my hand, and did what she wanted to do in her mind. She drew a beautiful heart shape inside that she wrote my name Hima. It looked nice especially because she gave freedom to that heart by adding wings to it. I liked it but said no in the beginning. She didn't fill my entire hand yet she made her wish. Unexpectedly Sravs leaned a bit forward to get a clear look at that, and made the thing messy. She held the place where my girl drew heart. This ruined our happiness. I gave an angry look at Sravs, and Sunanda had mixed feelings. She was angry at the same time her happiness went down with this accident. The cute girl with her mess couldn't make an eye contact with us, and left in shock saying sorry. Sunanda said it's ok, but we all knew it made us feel down. When I washed my hand, I saw that mehendi had left its stain and turned almost orange color. I showed it to them, and we cheered up again. These little memories are quite lovable, and put our hearts in solace.

Sunanda got an offer letter after relieving from B.Tech, in our college itself when I was in Hyderabad, her parents refused the offer as they can't send her far from them so she started preparing for CAT exams, she put many efforts to achieve another job, and stay with her family. She had many dreams to lead a beautiful, and peaceful life. She always wanted to prove herself as a good teacher. That's her favourite profession. She used to tell us in our college days about her dream to be a good teacher. She might have thought of all these when her health was getting bad, and so she told me.

This was the time Sravs, and Mouni got to know about Sunanda's condition, all were shocked knowing what was going on with her.

# 31

It was the 10th of July, 2020 Friday evening. I was back from my work, I saw her messages. It was the day that we had the worst conversation, it was filled with arguments carried away with pain. I thought of giving her happiness, which ended up making things messy. She is the girl I love the most. At the end of the day, I couldn't make her happy, and this guilt hits me every time. The discussion was so high that she left the SMSB group on WhatsApp, which we created during our college days. Later, I added her, and she left again, and the process continued. Then I thought not to vex her; I will call her the next morning.

As we had a very bad discussion, neither she nor I tried to talk to each other. It was my week off, and I watched movies, and spent the day with my family. Though I had an urge to talk to her, I didn't call her. The next day I was feeling sick, and slept on the bed, in the afternoon Sravs called me saying Sunanda was admitted in Vizag hospital, yesterday her condition grew worse as she couldn't bear the pain anymore, she was taken to a local hospital where unexpectedly she got fits, and the doctors advised her parents to take her Vizag as the situation was very critical, soon they reached the place, and admitted her in the hospital, on hearing this I forgot my pain, stood up, and asked how she was, to which she replied "We have to call aunty, and get further details." This was the time I thought of going there, and called my mom but she refused as the situation outside was very bad, she suggested me not to come, and everything is going to be alright. I cried, and called back to Sravs. We talked to aunty who was depressed like anything.

On hearing us, she couldn't resist her tears, and said, "What is happening to your friend? She is not even in conscious. Uncle is completely feeling bad, and is not talking to anyone; he became so pale. Some of our relatives are here, and we are managing." She disconnected my phone to get Sunanda's dressing changed as per the nurse advice. Sravs tried to make me calm down, I told her about the fight that we had, and she said we too had such an argument. I wanted to go, and tell Sunanda that we are there for her, and things are going to be set right, but I couldn't. I wanted to see her, talk to her, and hug her until our pain vanishes. Our sister was alone in the house, so she later went to her grandparent's home. No one was able to sleep that night.

We used to call Srija daily, and learn about Sunanda's health condition. Days were getting worse; I couldn't sleep or eat, but just imagine the condition of her parents. They were getting more, and more panicky while seeing their daughter in bed. What about my girl? She was unable to wake up, and ask for something. What was the biggest mistake of her that she was lying there and being in that condition? Is it because she was accepting every pain, and acting like everything was normal in her life? The reason is unknown, and the only thing we know is to join our hands, pray, and pray, and think of the invisible bond that is going to make things normal. I don't know how well they were heard. Aunty said, “She is getting normal, let's hope for her speedy recovery.” With this, we had a normal rhythm in our heartbeats.

Hearing this news, I was extremely glad, and happy. I thought of seeing her once, and asked one of her cousins to make a video call, but as she was in the ICU, I couldn't see her. There was a rapid fluctuation with her reports; at a time, we got to know that she was getting better, and within no time, we used to get scared because of the change in her breath. She was on ventilators, and had a continuous oxygen supply as she couldn't breathe on her own. Slowly, she went into a coma. Hearing this in movies, which is just a word, still makes us feel the pain, though we know it was acting. When it comes to real life, seeing your loved ones in such a situation is not that easy. The person being alive means they are just alive but can't respond to a single action. My brain used to think several times, and be worried about her health, but my heart used to say that soon we were going to be happy.

One day I called her cousin, and asked how she was. She said, "Don't worry; the results are normal, and we can have a discharge soon, so don't bother anymore." Hearing this news, I felt like all our prayers were heard, and she is going back home. Later, I went to the office, and was having my lunch in the cafeteria, but all of a sudden, her thoughts distracted me. I could visualize how we ate together in the afternoons for those beautiful 4 years, and every happiest moment started playing in front of my eyes, but I was not feeling happy; some pain was killing me inside that I couldn't eat anymore. I walked out of the place, went to the lift lobby, and talked to aunty. She started crying, saying doctors were losing hope on her, and asked to take her home. I was shocked that morning itself her reports were normal, and how come again all these things were happening? She couldn't speak anymore, and ended the call.

The day was completely disturbed, and I felt so guilty for not being there at that time. I came back home in the late evening, and talked to Srija. She said, "Just now we got to know she is fine, and you people shouldn't worry." I really didn't know how to react, but being in a bit of positive news, I felt thankful to God inside. Sravs, Srija, and I talked for half an hour, and later I felt a bit stronger, and hoped for her speedy recovery.

Things are getting back to normal. She came back home, slowly regained her consciousness, and started identifying everyone. Within a few days post-lockdown, I went to see her. Just like normal days, I could hear her voice teasing her sister. I was standing outside the door, and upon seeing me after more than a year, approximately 14 months, she forgot her anger towards me. We stood opposite to each other for a while, and then she rushed towards me, and hugged me so tight that tears burst out of our eyes. The neighbors started giggling upon seeing us, and her mom shed happy tears. Srija ran towards us, and the three of us hugged each other. Uncle called us inside, and asked her to take rest as she was getting back to normal by then. We looked into each other's eyes, and couldn't stop crying. We managed ourselves into the home. We were silent for some time, and then laughed at each other, as if a big stand-up comedy had happened in front of us. We both had a great talk, which lasted the whole day, and we forgot to eat until aunty brought us something to eat. This was the time she kept on talking again, and just like those four years, I listened to her fascinating words in tranquility.

# 32

I wish this happened, I wish this is the ultimate happiness to stay with me until my last breath, but fate planned something so cruel that which I cannot imagine but it happened. It happened all of a sudden no one was in a position to believe this but people around me said it happened.

In that late evening after talking to Srija, and Sravani, I was happy to listen to their words, and the speedy recovery of Sunanda. Within no time I received a message from Sravs that I can't say because I'm unable to frame words for what I saw. I still remember how I was in that time, on seeing the message every part of my body started shivering, my eyes were unable to shut, I almost became senseless that I couldn't say a word, my phone was shivering as my hands were, my grandma was asking, "What's wrong why are you shivering so heavy?" I could hear everything, feel everything but was not in a position to respond to anything for a while. Slowly gaining consciousness, I called, and shouted at her, "What did you say?" She said some of her friends told her. I called Sunanda's cousin to make a confirmation just to prove what Sravs said was wrong. She picked the call, with a soft tone. I asked her, "She is okay right!" I couldn't hear a word. I asked her again, and again, and again just to say one thing. "Please tell me that she is okay. You said in the morning that everything is fine, and reports were normal so confirm to me once that she is fine now." She said something that was very devastating to hear, very hard to take, and cried saying "I can't tell you more than this, and I have no more words to say." I could feel tears rolling out of my eyes as the information already passed to my brain but the heart which was still not in a position to believe or convince itself, still pleading her to say that she is okay, she will be happy just like before but she didn't, her mom took phone, and said the same, my phone fell down, my grandma took the phone, and asked what happened, she explained her from the beginning, I was hearing that but couldn't talk more, I hung up the call, tears were not controlling, they were rolling down my cheeks continuously with no pause, thinking of her that was the first time I called out Nandu for more than an hour or two. I was just calling her name crying saying no, pleasing her, joining my hands so tight, I cried, and cried, and cried because I didn't know what to do further, my grandfather came in after being aware, he tried to console me but I couldn't. Later, he scolded me for being so childish. I didn't know how to react to his words, I was crying because I'm far away from the biggest happiness of my life, everything appeared pale, and colorless. I decided to go to her, and see her, told the same thing to everyone in the home but they disagreed because of the situation, and there was less transport facility available due to covid scenario. I said “I'm not going to stop anymore, and I have to go.” They argued a lot, and called my mom. I couldn't speak a word, just cried, and begged my mom to allow me to come there, and see her. As she understood my pain, she convinced my grandparents, and they agreed. I didn't know how to get there, through which transportation I should there. After gaining consciousness, I searched for flights but there were few, and that was the first time I searched for a flight just to reach to her soon. It didn't work out as I couldn't find anything because my brain was not in its presence, so I decided to go, and catch a train for which my grandparents agreed to send me the next morning as it was too late at night. They tried to make me come out of it but that was highly impossible because I can't have a deviation from her, I was thinking of her, the fight which we had, and blamed myself as I cried out, I didn't know where to stop, how to get deviated but was screaming in pain, a pain which I never experienced in my life as of then. My family members were worrying because I was completely losing myself to that pain. I thought of gaining myself but I couldn't. After a long time consoling myself, I stopped crying then everyone slept, I opened my eyes looking blank into the vacuum but couldn't speak, couldn't cry out aloud, hiding pain, and crying within which was actually a hell, the pain I was suffering from was killing me, and to hide my tears without coming out was the other hell. I was thinking of her going into those memories. I slept for two to three hours, and woke up all of a sudden, looked around, felt very numb, and again tears started rolling down. It was 4 o'clock in the morning, I put my legs down the bed, and all of sudden a thought struck my brain saying you are going to walk alone from today. I managed myself to get up, and freshen up, wore the same orange dress which I wore on the last day of college unexpectedly and later realized that I have her memories with that dress as well. I woke my brother up as my family suggested that I should go with him because going out alone in such a crisis is not good. We took the bag which was packed by my grandma, and my brother bid bye to them but my grandpa was angry at me as I was doing such a thing, I felt bad that it was the first time I crossed him as none of our family member did it before then.

But I had no option. I apologized within, and left the place. I took the money I had which I saved to buy a phone, and as she said we will be having our picture on the back case. It started raining slowly. We booked an auto, and went to the railway station. We tried to get in but some people stopped us at the entrance itself asking for reservation which we didn't have as we started unexpectedly. I pleaded to the policeman to allow us in but he didn't as it was Covid time. There were no general tickets, and I had to wait until the afternoon to get a reservation for which I didn't have that time. When we got to know that this won't work out, we thought of going to bus station, and took an auto to catch-up the bus, but no driver was going to the bus station, I scolded my own destiny, and after a while we caught an auto, and he said there were no buses available at that time, and suggested to catch a car which was actually available at that time as no other road transport was there to cross the state. We reached city outskirts, booked a cab, and was waiting to start. That driver didn't start the vehicle as one of the passengers was not there, I didn't know either to scold him or blame myself that it was being late, and I had to reach her. It took more than half an hour for him to start the vehicle, that half an hour was like a hell that I couldn't step ahead of or go back, and catch another source which I didn't have anyways. That was the day I got to know the value of every single second passed was that precious, and that tragic. While studying, and in lecturers giving speeches, I heard that time is valuable, and once lost we can't go back to a single second. I experienced that. I suddenly felt an urge to go back in time, if possible, through a time machine as we see in science fiction just to see her once, and stay with her forever. As long as life sticks in the body I don't know how much we love a person but once it enters all the universe free we love them more than anything.

# 33

The car started moving after a long horrible wait, Sravs called me in the meanwhile, and I said I'm coming to see her, she said why now as the virus is spreading all round, and now her family members are taking her home, and she will be alright, with those words for a while I was happy, and confused. It means that she is recovering again, and this thought put some hope to life back again, by her family members statements I completely felt that I couldn't see or talk to her anymore, and when I got to know that she was provided with oxygen, and doctors will be treating her, again thoughts of hope, and happiness started blooming, I was traveling chanting the Maha mrutyumjaya mantra with a deep connection towards her. I don't know how many gods I prayed for her life, I just asked them to make her healthy, and let her be happy. It was around 10 o'clock when Sravs called me, and said you can't see her anymore, it's better you go back. It means we are going to face the darkest side of our lives. Everything froze in my head, unable to understand what these people were saying. They say she is fine, again, they call back, and say you can't see her anymore. It was raining heavily outside, there was a long empty, and beautiful road with flowers all around. Everything suddenly started becoming pale to my eyes, I leaned back, and stared outside just couldn't feel anything happening around me. Tears were rolling down, and my brother sitting beside me didn't know what to say, neither before he saw me like that nor I faced such pain. All of a sudden there was a brake on the car but not on my thoughts this time. I was completely engaged in her memories, how those four years were, and what was the situation I was facing, I was unable to deviate myself, I was in pain, a pain which can't be soothed, and healed.

Something very hard stuck my heart, it was more painful like an arrow from a bow hit me directly to the heart from far sight, the pain was more than a slaughter, my heart was beating asynchronously thinking what happened, and was it real, where am I going now, to see what, and is there any way I can get back to her. I don't know but I just traveled, every second reminded me of her words. I recollected one of her recent words that she said you won't come to me even whatever happens to me, and these words put a slap on my face, feeling guilty why didn't I reach her before at least when she was in the hospital. Had I been there she would have been talking to me, and her family right now. My touch, my pain, my love, and the bond we have would definitely make her gain consciousness but I didn't do that. I felt that my bond was weak so I couldn't save her! Why didn't I take a step forward just like today previously? This sin was killing me inside, and the anger out of the pain couldn't be expressed, crying out loud inside.

The driver was having breakfast, and we couldn't move. I didn't know to whom I should show my frustration or should I be quiet, I was hardly able to speak out. Again, trying for flights, and seeing the weather I got to know how unlucky I was. I have not even crossed hundreds of kilometres. Sravs called me, and said she will be going to Sunanda's home, and I pleaded her to let me see her one time, and please wait for me. She said she will try asking Sunanda's family members, and called me back saying, "As these days were not good, they are taking her soon, and can't wait until you come." What should be my reaction? I lost my last hope to see her. The thought of not being able to see her anymore, not being able to touch, and hug her anymore was becoming more, and even worse. I was unable to bear the pain but still with the thought of seeing her for the last time made me move ahead. The Covid directly didn't attack us but indirectly it was taking our lives. I was looking at the road but was unable to see anything as my eyes were full of tears, unable to judge what's going on around me, and where I could see her further. I started looking around with a thought that she would be around me. My soul started wandering where she could be, could I touch her, talk to her, and beg her to wake up for me and look at me.

I was getting to know that I can't see her but my heart was not ready to accept that, and it was trying to reach her. As it was Covid if we go via main roads, we need to take Covid test at toll gates, and we were not supposed to cross the state if someone in the vehicle gets tested positive, all the people would be under quarantine for 14 days, so, we took shortcut. There was no one else on that road, it was not even constructed, having full of farms, I looked into them, and remembered traveling with her through such roads. I asked Sravs to let me see her through video call but she didn't take her mobile there, and I didn't know whom I could call, and ask anything. I was thinking she would have reached home but not just like before. I was thinking of her parents, and our sister. How could that little girl take this? I couldn't think of her going away from us. How unfair is this? Why all this was happening with her, I don't know.

After traveling for more than six hours we reached Vijayawada. We went to the bus station, and booked an immediate reservation for another bus, and waited for it. We waited there for more than two hours, and I asked my brother to eat something as he also didn't eat anything but he refused. In the meanwhile, my mom called me, and asked where we were. She tried to console me, and was also worried about us at the same time. I was numb by that time, tears stopped in my eyes. I said I was okay. Saying okay when we are not is really another level of deep pain. In these two hours everything was completed at her place, and even thinking of that I didn't know how to react, I was able to visualize what pain, and unbearable things going over there, I was quietly looking at time. Every second that moved forward, and the time lapse from second to second made me think of all the old sayings regarding time. I just want to force those needles back to where she can live along with me or at least make her live at her place.

Slowly, I got to know everything that happened, and moving forward I will just live, live in a world where beauty, and happiness are lost. There will be no more happiest things that I can have with her, I can't see her beautiful face, I can't listen her, I can't tease her neither can she. There will be no more cute, and long conversations, fights, laughter, anything. I didn't know in what phase of life I was in, and what the hell was I doing there, where, and for whom I was going? No answers for the questions but wanted to go to the place where she was at least as of then.

Again, we started moving in a bus from Vijayawada to Vizag. I took my seat, and we were traveling. My brother seemed tired, and he was sleeping. I looked at him, and thought that I was bothering him. There was continuous run of movies in the front seat, and looking at them I felt these were the films that released when she was there with me though we didn't see them together. It was such a long journey, I was engaged in her thoughts, and tears started running out of my eyes again. I was not even thinking of anything at some points but I didn't know why tears were rolling down. I felt like hating this distance between us, I just wanted to rush towards her, and hug her just like that.

It was 11 in the midnight, we reached Vizag a day before where she was there in that city, it was just a matter of 12 hours, half a day everything changed in our lives. Soon entering the city, gave me a thought of being with her, the breath she had taken a few hours ago, and the same air in which she was there. It made me think I was being with her. I know just to satisfy myself my brain is thinking all that but has no other option. We got to know that the city is going to be under lockdown as cases were rising, and people coming from other places were supposed to be under quarantine there itself, getting to know about this my parents, and family members started worrying for us where as I thought of my destiny, I could reach to a place where she was there before some hours, and a night before.With five hours remaining, I thought about going to see her, but I was unable to do so, even though I had already arrived at more than half of my target. I sat at a place, and realized, that was the place where I was sitting with her a year ago when we went to the beach. I touched the place, stood at the place where she was, went to the washroom where we both had a funny conversation when I was applying face wash, the way she teased me, everything was visible to my eyes. I didn't know what to do, and where to go. I closed my eyes, felt those days memories, and sat at the places where she sat to feel her, I was able to reach until that place where I had few memories with her, post that if I go forward everything is under pain, and she took me up to the happiest place just to console me, I got to know I can't move forward. I opened my eyes, looked everything around again thinking of our moments at that place, and started back again to Hyderabad. I didn't know what I did, what I had in my mind. We just got into another bus after an hour at 12 o' clock, and were moving in an opposite direction which was quite unexpected just like the day.

# 34

Once we got on the bus it was almost midnight. My brother became so weak as he didn't have anything since morning. He ate a piece of cake which he bought from a store, and forced me to eat, I was not feeling hungry. As he was not eating, I took a bite which I swallowed very hard. He slept after the bus started moving. I didn't understand why I was going back all of a sudden, the announcement regarding lockdown, and what was all that happened around me. Soon the bus started moving from the place, I felt as if I was going far away from her. I closed my eyes but, unable to fall asleep, turned side to side. I was stuck in her thoughts completely. After traveling some distance, the bus stopped due to some engine issue, it was not starting. I observed the driver, and everyone getting down doing all the stuff to start the engine again. I turned aside looking through the window, and soon I could see a person or a shape of such kind out of the window in that darkness. It was just like a spark with something appearing like an outline, the spark was all around in complete white shine. I didn't know what that was, I woke my brother up, and asked him if he could see anything but he said nothing, just dark. We stuck there for more than twenty minutes, and I could see that as long as we were there, and all of a sudden it just faded away. I thought it was an illusion but not sure that an illusion lasts for more than twenty minutes even after the other person says that he couldn't see. My eyes were tired of crying, and they closed, and went to sleep. I saw her in my dream talking to me but I didn't remember what she said, she was just smiling looking at me. Soon I woke up, and looked around. I got to know that I dreamt of her, and tried to figure out what she said but I couldn't. I was just looking out in pale. The other morning, we reached Rajahmundry, and from there we caught another bus, and traveled up to Vijayawada where we had a break, and I charged my phone, talked to my mom, she said in a soft tone, "Go safe, and don't worry everything is going to be alright." I'm not convinced with her second statement as nothing was going right which I was experiencing for more than 24 hours.

Later we booked a car, and started moving towards Hyderabad. Before that whenever I traveled, I used to love the long roads but as of then I could see nothing, no beauty, no happiness. I was looking at the clouds in the Sky thinking if mythology is true, she might be looking at me, and her beloved ones from there. I was not ready to accept that thought, and looked down where I saw flowers throughout the road thinking that she had bloomed in this form but getting the thought of the next day I stopped looking outside, and closed my eyes where I could see her smiling at me just like in my dream. Tears rolled down slowly. I opened my eyes, and again the chain repeated from Sky to vacuum. I didn't know where to escape, what the situation I was in, and was getting to know that's what the real pain is. It took us more than five hours to reach Hyderabad. Once we reached home my grandparents were happy seeing me, and my brother coming safe. I went in, and locked the door, put all the dresses that were in the bag out, started wandering here, and there, trying to engage myself in something so that I couldn't think of her but this thought put me in great pain, and I sat down crying, and crying aloud with which my pain should go out but I had to cry low else they would get to know about my condition. Slowly, I gathered courage within, and got freshen up still tears were rolling from my eyes, and wiped them with towel, came out just normal. By that time, I felt hungry, and ate enough, I again went into the room saying, “I need some rest.” The hardest part started when I tried to control the tears which is actually too difficult but still managed, and tried to handle the pain.

# 35

Suddenly everything changed around me, I felt alone, I missed her, I missed her company, her love, her voice, her touch, is it true what I was thinking? I couldn't believe anything, I didn't know what all was happening around me, I felt tired, and fell asleep, every time I slept, I could see her as if she was talking to me in real life. Maybe that's true but when I opened my eyes, I felt that emptiness. I stood in the balcony saw two squirrels fighting, and having fun with each other, they were playing hide, and seek, there was only one squirrel visible, I couldn't see the other one, I didn't know why this impacted me so emotionally, I kept on looking for the latter to join the first squirrel. After a long time, they both met, and started squeaking which gave me a big solace. The thought of being distant was killing me inside, the worst thing is that I couldn't share the pain with anyone, I could tell her but I was not able to see her or talk to her. I was the one who told her once to share feelings with some loved ones, but I couldn't do it because she is the one for me to share all the details. My friends called, and tried to comfort me, but I couldn't come out of her. In the evening, Nani called me, and said that he would send me her photos as I was not able to see her. I requested Sravs for one picture so she told him, and he sent me her pics before doing so, he warned me, and requested me not to cry or not to panic. I said, "I won't please send it."

I saw a pop-up from him, he sent me her last pics, I opened the chat with my eyes half closed, not daring to see but have to see, gathered all my courage, and saw it. I didn't cry, I didn't utter a word, I just saw it in a full frame. She was lying on the ground, and sleeping, she was in deep sleep with no movement. She was draped with some clothes around her. I could see her hand was out of the coverage, touched her hand, and stuck there for a while, I slowly looked up, and zoomed towards her face which was the biggest pain but saw her, and touched her face. She was having Kumkum on her forehead, and as a part of ritual she had dung on her forehead, pain is hitting inside. Her lips were a bit moved front as she had her food through pipes, and had oxygen supply when she was in the hospital, they were dry, and pale. I don't know why I was seeing her so deeply. Maybe because, I cannot see her again, but I didn't like to see her in that situation. I didn't want to look but I was touching her saying this is not you, what my eyes were seeing was false, and a big lie that shouldn't happen even in a dream. I touched her long hair, and remembered how beautiful she looked when she had loose hair but not this time, it was completely wet, and was touching the ground. I zoomed out the picture, she was having a pink saree over her which was glittering full, and she was completely with flowers garland over her neck. This was not at all fair; I was dying within my heart to see that but was looking at that for some time feeling so numb. I didn't cry. I closed my phone, and called Nani. He asked if I was okay. I said yes, and hung up the call. I roamed here, and there thinking of touching the phone but having her pictures of that condition stopped me. My friends asked me to delete it but I didn't. When they said if you want to believe that happened, keep it or else just delete, I soon deleted that from chat, album, and even from Google photos just not to have a thought of losing her. I sat in my room thinking of nothing but something. I was not feeling good but tried to act normal for which my heart was not allowing me, in all the thoughts somewhere I lost. I didn't want to eat but forcefully ate a bit, and went away from the place, and sat in my room. During the night, I was not getting any sleep. Somewhere in the midnight when my eyes got strained, they fell to sleep but in that I saw her talking to me about something, saying many things, and when I opened my eyes they were completely filled with tears.

Seeing me like that, Sravs, Mouni, and my friends tried to call me but if someone tried to call me, I didn't pick up the phone, I gave it to my family, and made them say I was sleeping. This happened, and then one evening they called me altogether, and made me remember all her good things. The thought of a smile was not there as it was resisted by my pain. I cried in my heart when they called me, I said, "I'll call back." I didn't want to engage with them because the conversation made me miss her. The thought of her not being there in conference literally killed me inside. Days were passing, I saw clock, and thought like hours before she was there, a day before she was there, a week ago she was there, a month ago she was there, and what if I go to past to my college days, I'll stick with her again, hug her, talk to her, enjoy, and live every single second of life. I somehow lost belief in almost everything, I used to pray to God, I stopped doing that, I didn't want to talk to God or ask to do something. Is it because I'm angry with him? At first, I thought it was completely his mistake, and felt like not to look at him, after time being, I felt it was my bane that I couldn't see her, why to blame others even God? For some reason I felt I'm a sinner, and I have no right to question him.

My family tried to make me come out of her thoughts, my friends did so, she is not a memory in my life that I can come out of, she is my happiness, my pain receiver, my adviser, my family without whom I can't imagine my life. Changing from one room to another diverts the thinking process in general yet when the agony is high nothing changes one's feelings. I don't remember what I did the whole day but sat alone, and went into trauma. I remember, during my childhood, one day I saw a bird dying in front of my eyes, it hurt me in that little age to see some life going away in front of my naked eyes, I asked my mom, and she said it is life, and it ends one day. I was not ready to accept her words instead I accused God for taking it away from its parents, I showed my anger for some hours by not talking to him, and not offering the prayers. Slowly I started realizing the ecosystem which I got to know in one of my classes that in order to sustain an ecosystem, and to maintain a balanced life cycle every living being has to die as it will help to maintain a balance environment. I accepted it, and realized myself. When it comes to a matured life at this age, I'm not ready to accept but swinging there itself, and I feel sometimes it's not maturity levels, its connection towards some people that will not let you out of the situation. For me, it's not a situation, at least I don't see it like that, I have a major connection, and bond with her that I can't let her out of my life.

# 36

I remembered that my dad used to take me to school on his scooter which was famous in those days, TVS. I felt high sitting on it as my hairs used to blow along with the air. When it comes to college, I had a group of friends with a very big bus to go on. Now, working as an employee all these were replaced with posh cars, and when it's too late at night, I have an escort deployed. These memories came into picture out of nowhere, and I thought this is what success looks like, and then it gives a big bang to everyone in its possible way, for me I lost that happiness with her. Looking perfect outside, lost the soul inside. I am thankful for the step-by-step growth, and success in my life but now something affects me much more, and this pain undertakes all the other comforts and luxuries that may come in my life. I used to ask my dad, "What is time, and what is the need of its measurements?" He replied as simply as possible saying time is in which we travel, and is measured in hours, minutes, and seconds. Now, I feel this is wrong. For everyone, time doesn't have this sophisticated meaning. Time is the phase in which one spends the happiest, and the most painful moments and in between it just swings on cheering, and hurting, and gaining back again to let one go into its flow.

It was one Monday morning which meant I had to go to the office. I woke up early, helped my grandmother in the kitchen, and started in my cab towards the office. Every day I board my cab I used to call her, I looked at my mobile opened dial tab typed her number, looked at it, and didn't understand what if she doesn't pick my call, maybe our sister is going to tell hold on I'll call her, and shout just like every time or aunty is going to pick the call, and ask about my safety, and give it to her. I put the phone back, looked out into the Sky thinking is she really going to see me from there or not, all of sudden I heard one of the songs that we used in our TikToks. I couldn't control my tears, they filled in my eyes. I felt like she gave me an indication that she is listening to me. The thought of distance was once just a word but now it is the biggest pain, and nothing became that painful later.

Within a month one of her cousins was blessed with a baby girl, all the family members thought that it was she who came back again. When I got to know about this, I felt happy at least with this some pain will go away from their mind by seeing the little one. I felt that it was she who came back again, unable to stay away from her family. She may not be the one but the thought of her re-birth made the whole family gain back again with some hope towards their lives yet the pain lasts forever.

# 37

Our cab used to pass beside a graveyard. I don't know why from my childhood when I look at it, I feel like watching inside very keenly what the place is, and how it would be like, it is not any stupidity but an interest or whatever it is, I just look inside. But this time, when I saw it from a far distance, I felt the physical loss of her, I was scared, the thought of her, and the day when happiness left our lives made me rewind the day when she was lying on the ground without conscious on the casket. I thought how painful it was for her dad to take her to that place, and do those rituals, how he put her on those sticks, he suffered to see her like that, and the thought made me suffer too. His dreams, and happiness went away along with the fire, and he took the deepest pain seeing her vanishing in front of his eyes. I visualized how everything happened with her which was not supposed to happen, even in a dream we never thought of but it became reality. I thought how destiny changed our lives, filling the utmost grief from which all her loved ones can't be completely happy later on. The thought of non-existence of physical presence chopped my heart into pieces, and the pain is inexpressive.

It took me just a week to make me strong enough but before that her name made me cry but then one night I saw her in my dream, she was not feeling good as we were not, I woke up with a determination not to cry, a few days passed, and I talked to aunty, she couldn't control herself, and said uncle was completely depressed with a thought that his negligence ended up like this, I tried to console her which I couldn't but still managed, and told her about my dream, requested them not to cry which they can't as I myself can't control so, how can I expect them to do, yet I tried. To come out of her thoughts I tried a few ways, but nothing worked out. I went through her chat, and read how silly conversations we had every time, a curve of a smile appeared, soon pain started within, and this is when I got to know memories make us cry one day. In the chat I found a book cover page with her name written on it, so I sent to her one day, when I was in the mall. I asked, "Why do you come wherever I go?" to which she replied "Two bodies one soul right?" I googled the book which was written by

Sunanda Mehta. When I started reading it, I found some situations, and conversations in the book just like we had in our lives. I started reading books with the thought that they would distract me from her thoughts but they didn't. Instead I fell more, and more into her. I started chatting with her in the group that she once created only for two of us on 14/07/2018 to have some fun. Later she left the group when she was angry upon me. I'm still in that group, and didn't know that for this day she created it for me. When I opened the history, it was a day before she created it for us, and after two years, I was like this to chat with her alone.

Nothing healed me to come out of her then I understood she herself can make me regain, she herself is my healing power. I started sharing my thoughts with her, how was my day, how things happen around me just like any other day. I started asking, and replying as if she was standing beside me, I told her something, and asked to say yes or no to which I got a reply in some source, and felt she is there with me, listening to me, and if I cry that will make her feel guilty. During college days when I cried, she used to go away from me, and later used to say, "I can't see you crying as it kills me inside." Remembering those days, I prepared myself to all the extent, I'm not missing her but I miss her, you know pain was hidden deep inside which I sealed, and pleaded myself to behave normal, and go on. I started believing things until they become real, as long as we believe something exists, it exists. I started believing as if she is listening, and yes, she does. Later, every pain seemed normal, and nothing hurt that much as I survived the utmost pain in my life. Still, I scold her, talk to her, play jokes on her, and in return I laugh feeling like she's enjoying, and having fun. In the beginning for a month, I used to be scared with the thought of what if she comes to me, and threatens me just as fun. Later, I got used to the thought of her presence, and now I enjoy her company just like in those beautiful four years of our B.Tech life. Hiding pain within, and living as everything is normal is actually a tough thing to do, whenever I see a girl wearing spectacles, dressing color combination that she has, the length of her hair, everything makes me see her everywhere. I just simply stare at the moment, and close my eyes. Losing a friend whom you love the most is not that easy in one's life, and to regain is the toughest battle I face every day. The person who teases you, and loves you is not there beside you means you lost the strength of your life but achieving something, and facing life back is when comes the actual strength of that person, and can be dedicated again back to that person. "I wait for you as though nature waits for warmth from the Sun." I told her.

After six months, I planned to go to her home to visit her parents, and sister in January. I went via bus, and the roads reminded me of that dark morning, once I reached Vizag, I started visualizing her moments again, I walked the path that she walked two years ago, stopped at a shop where she bought a chain, searched for the similar one but couldn't find it. It is a four-hour journey to my home from Vizag. After having my breakfast, I caught a bus, and it started moving. Unconsciously, I again felt pain remembering that day, though I controlled myself, tears were rolling down. Six months ago, when I tried to move ahead from the place, I was not able to cross that point but today I was going ahead, it seemed someone pre-planned that I shouldn't move forward on that day. Something stopped me then, if I were there when she was in hospital, she would have been alright today, our bond, my physical presence in front of her, my touch would have made her stay back with me but why this didn't happen? so many thoughts were running in my head. I visualized that she traveled through this place when going back home in an ambulance, I started feeling her breath around me, I cried throughout the journey remembering her, I tried to control but they were flowing down. Once I reached Bobbili, I saw a way to go to Parvathipuram, and a way to Balijipeta, her place, and mine. Memories were killing me deep inside again, that we wandered here, and there. I took an auto, and continued my journey, this is a journey where I had complete memories of us, the roads we walked, the shops, restaurants, ice cream parlor, I crossed everything, I saw her everywhere, I was getting near to the college, our college is on the way towards my journey. In the meanwhile, an old woman sitting beside me asked me who's the girl on your mobile back cover. I printed one of our selfies on the back cover which she told me earlier. I told her that she's my friend. She said, "She looks much like you, and I thought she is your sister so where does she live?" on which I held my breath for a while, and replied "In Parvathipuram." "Oh, that's very near you can see her whenever you want" she said, and I said nothing, just put a smile on my face thinking yes very near that one day I'm going to see her, and I will wait for that day. Before our college there is another college where we had our last exams, and that's the place where I went away from her when she was not able to leave my hand. My thoughts stopped at the place for a while, moving forward I saw our college which is not only a place of college but also a place where our bond originated. I looked at the classroom which was visible from far a sight, looked at entire college in a glance, and thought of those beautiful memories. I was not sure how many plenty of memories we had over there but every place is a place of happiness. I reached home, and freshened up, even my home is filled with her memories, the days she was there, cracking jokes, and complaining to my mom about me. Sravs called me in the evening, and asked me to come to her home. Soon after that dark day that happened in our lives, Sravs got engaged, and in January she got married, I didn't attend it, how could I? We all planned to have lots of fun during our marriages but didn't expect this shock. Sravs requested me to come but I didn't have that courage, and moreover, I would spoil her happiness so, I made an excuse saying, "I have lot of office work and getting leaves approved would be impossible." I know I hurt her but it would be better for her also or else we end up in sad mood even on an important day in her life. Somehow, I managed myself, and sent Haldi function saree, and the bridal flower jewelry through one of her friends, and made the day beautiful enough stating it was sent to her as per Sunanda's wish as she loves crafting items, and functions a lot. I said I'll meet her some day after visiting Sunanda's family as Sravs was at her in-law's home.

After three days, one Sunday me, and Nani went to her home. The route was very tough for me to travel. I was talking to him as we met after a year but it would have been a more beautiful moment if we had gone there just like every time. We went to a sweet shop, and bought some sweets as my mom told me to buy, and we were in their street. I remembered that one day when I was at Sunanda's home, she took me to a shop, I saw it, and moving forward I was becoming so tense not understanding what a day I was in. I saw her home from far sight, slowly reaching there as the distance was fading away, my heart was becoming very weak yet gathered strength within thinking that I'm supposed to heal them not to end them up in misery, Nani said the same. I saw aunty sitting outside, she became very weak, her face was so tired that I can understand she hardly slept at night. Seeing me her eyes became wet, I never saw her like that. She always had a smile on her face, hugged us when we went there, and used to mingle with us which we enjoyed. I took her hand, and we walked in. The house is engaging in her as if she was talking to me. Aunty couldn't control her tears, she was sobering out of pain, I didn't know how to handle her but managed saying, "Aunty please." Only that I could say, I had no words because I myself was not able to bear that, how come a mother manages herself. I tried to distract her but she didn't. Then our sister came, she saw me, and hugged me asking how I was? We talked for a while. She is so brave, and built herself so much stronger than me as she had to look after her parents. I liked her spirit but somewhere she lost after a while hugged me so tight, and cried out. I lost my courage, and tears rolled down, I walked out of the room, and soon Nani went to aunty, and consoled her. I cried hard saying no, Nani called me in, again I managed, and sat beside them, aunty asked about me after a while, and we had some conversation. She said, "I know how much pain you hide within; I can understand" for which I had no words, and later said, "No, I'm okay." Sunanda, and me tried to buy bangles for her mom as it was her birthday, she selected online order, and paid me the amount to buy it but somehow, we couldn't give her as there was an order mismatch so I took those bangles when I went to her home, and said, "It was your daughter's wish to present them to you, please wear them." She cried on seeing those bangles, I put them on her hands, and she looked at them with utmost love. She kept on saying about that day, how she was hospitalized. "The last days were unbearable that she had everything through pipes, she was in ICU, her brain stopped functioning. She was in continuous observation, set on ventilators, couldn't move her hand as it was covered with an IV set." She was telling me how much torture she faced, the girl who was very scared of an injection, and used to cry seeing one, was completely set in emergency room. I thought of the pain she had that day, and how much she would have suffered then. I thought of her while aunty was telling the pain she had gone through, I should have been there to make her regain but I wasn't, the pain made me cry. "After being in coma she still gave response to some treatments which gave confidence that everything is going to be fine, as on doctors advise we planned to take her home in the ambulance before which doctors made a cut through her neck side for the supply of oxygen, and set a pipe over there but in the middle of journey, I saw her taking her last breaths." said her mother. The most painful phase she came across, and it's not easy for a mother to see her beloved child in that situation, the pain lasts forever. The thought of having a cut through her neck, and seeing all that was another big punishment.

Being a mother, giving birth, nourishing the child and seeing them grow becomes the happiest part of a mother's life but seeing that child taking last breath gives an infinite pain to her and she also loses her life there itself. I stopped speaking, held her hand said nothing, we left in silence which was cracked by our sister, and managed her mom to come out of that, soon we tried to deviate her, and aunty asked us to eat lunch to which we denied, I looked at her home completely, saw all her crafts which were in the cupboards, and her photos, I saw one near prayer room. I went upstairs along with our sister, and saw her photo frame which was dusted, I wiped out the dust on it, looked at all the photos, and a frame that we presented her was hanged in reverse, when I asked our sister, she said, "Mom was looking at them not having food so we turned them to the other side, now you can put in normal as she is far better." I put the frame there, looked around, memorized those beautiful, and unforgettable days of our lives, and went down. I took the photo out of the prayer room, and hugged the photo frame cried out saying sorry, I hugged aunty, and sister, and later left the place.

After reaching home, I slept beside my mom, hugged her, and cried silently. A mother knows her child's pain, though I cried in silence she understood my pain, and soothed me. A few days later, I met all my childhood friends who live near me, and came back to Hyderabad. I didn't meet any other from our gang, and it was a long time that I hadn't talked to many of the people from college, I just had no courage to meet them at that time.

# 38

The view on life changed with her, my thought process, handling a situation everything was changed. The time that passed would never come back I know, because I have experienced that with her. The way I walk slowly gave me confidence that she's walking beside me just like the previous days, and it gave me a hope to face the world. At times, I talk to her out so loud just like normal because I can feel her presence in some senses. I somehow lost my interest in drinking tea as once I told her, "In our next meeting, you are going to prepare chai, and offer it to me." Before then I stopped drinking tea as I wanted to adopt a new lifestyle but this somehow changed me to not to have any more again in future. I started watching Big Boss seasons just to know what the characters are, and how they made her happy that she discussed even during classes. The watch that she gave me in our first year was completely broken, but I always had it in my bag. I took it to a nearby watch shop, and asked him to repair it. He looked at me for a while, and then took the watch. Nothing was working, the belt was apart, the battery was dried-up, and the seconds needle was so delicate, he said better you take one more watch rather than repairing this to which I denied. He asked me, "Was this gifted?" I nodded my head, he said, "Then you can ask that person to present you a new one right!" I smiled, and said, "It is my first gift from my friend, and I want this to be good enough, and work properly just like before." He asked for two days as he found the crown part was missing. After two days he said, "Better you search in home for the spare part as this is an old watch, I couldn't find a spare for this." The day I went to my home-town I searched for something in my bag but unexpectedly I found its spare, and was extremely delighted that I had the watch with me, and this spare part was hidden in my bag. After reaching Hyderabad, I gave the watch with its spare to the watch mechanic, he remembered me, and asked where I found it, I said, "At my hometown." He might have thought how important the watch is for me so he didn't question me further this time. He took it, and repaired it. Later, one day I went to him, and he fixed the belt of the watch, and needle properly making sure it won't fall down due to its movement. He attached the spare part, and made a fine finish with silver coating which was paled out earlier. I took it with utmost happiness thinking that every movement of a second needle makes me feel her presence again. But again, it was dried up and the belt was apart, to repair it again it needs to be replaced with new parts so, I didn't want to repair this time because the watch she gave me will be completely replaced with new ones for which my heart didn't accept.

When I read her diaries, I saw how safely she kept my ten rupees note that I threw with a pack of chocolates while going to Hyderabad. When I saw her for the first time, I thought that she was the happiest girl. Later, when I traveled along with her in her footsteps, I got to know that she was the utmost pain receiver that I met in my life. When we had fights in the last days, she used to get furious, and tried to get away from me, I didn't know then that she was doing that for my sake so I can't miss her later just like she did in our college. I thought of not talking to her for one day, and never expected that a single day would last for a complete life span distance in our lives. Just like heart transplantation, and kidney dialysis if we had a technology, and innovation to bring back life, I wouldn't have lost her today. I always felt that she should have a bright future, and I wished to see her grow as high as possible in her life but never knew that today I'll see her with Sky as limit.

People say there exist seven identical facial features. If that's true, I wish I could see at least one of the other six faces. As per one of the sayings, regrets are stronger than gratitude, maybe somewhere deep inside I feel myself as a sinner that I haven't met her in those days, and this regret would kill me till my lifetime. When I talked to her, hundreds of kilometeres just faded away with an illusion of soul, coming to the present, maybe I can't see her but I will see her soon, maybe I can't hear her but I will hear her soon, I'll find her, and I'll meet her. When a flower blooms I imagine that it is her rebirth, accept it, and wait for the next day to bloom again, no other thoughts of suppression, only a sense of consolation. When two friends yell at each other, and make fun I can hear that sarcasm from her, that's how we used to have fun. I laugh very loud imagining these things yet the pain lasts forever. My eyes can sense that I'm unable to see her still, my heart says that I'm going to see her sooner or later. When I see an ambulance pass beside me, my imagination comes into picture thinking she had been just like that in one of the ambulances suffering pain, it leads to a different level of trauma that I couldn't inhale properly, I stop my breath for few seconds, and hope that this breath would add some extra life to the person in ambulance so that no one could face the suffering just like we do. I'm not sure what all precious memories I will have more or had long back, I won't regret the same loss for other memories because this hurt killed me more than anything else. I wanted to know the pain she suffered, and in the beginning I researched about her conditions, and what all she had gone through, the written over text in wiki made my heart feel drenched through invisible tears that I stopped to read further, and yes, she is the strongest woman who faced physical, and mental issues more than her experience at that little age. One thing is she remained youthful forever, and there is no need to worry about her skin care, ageing issues, she looked as beautiful as I saw her the very first time. One knows the value of life when another's ends. It happened in my life, and I was cursed to live a life without complete happiness. It hurt me so much that after a while I couldn't feel it as if it became rock solid.

Create as many memories as possible because one day we won't be satisfied with few memories.

I'm afraid that if I grew older, and there's a day when I can't remember some of these beautiful memories though they are very close to my heart, but maybe some aging stuff makes days different, and hence I found a way to put the memories down in this book so they become eternal. One day, when I reach her she'll show me the entire new world just like she did in B.Tech, makes me feel jealous by staying close to some other then she hugs me tight that we last into it for a long while. "For the never-ending Sky the Moon becomes the beauty spot, and for this long running life you are always my happy Moon."

"When my hands were in yours, fingers used to grab each other so quickly but now I can feel the distance between them, and how spacious they are. Seeing this, happiness won't be eternal. The eyes that gaze into the vacuum let me know how it feels." I feel my fingers on her cheeks when I look at some pics, and she has very soft cheeks now when I look at my fingers, I miss that touch. Previously, she used to talk, and I used to listen to her happiness, and pain but it's vice versa as of today. I want those days to come back into my life when she would again speak to me which is a bit hard yet she satisfies my wishes by appearing in dreams. The calendar paper that swings to, and fro gives me a count of days that are passing, and her birthday is coming soon, slowly I prepared myself not to cry, and engage in her memories. I remember how she slept the night when I was in her home without taking her spectacles off, and her sister slowly came towards her, took them away, and without them also she looked adorable. I feel within myself, and try to get back into sleep where I can engage in her memories. The wind that touches my face reminds me of her presence in a way that it feels like she is coming towards me. Watching the dark Sky with the Stars, and the Moon was the biggest visual treat I had since childhood. Ignoring the Sky now my eyes fall on one of the Star that looks brighter, thinking she is saying something to me. When I was going for her that day, I found an eyelash on my hand, I held it strong made a wish of her speedy recovery, and blew it off, this was one of my wishes making come true since childhood, days later when I saw another on my hand, I felt it useless to do so, and I stopped believing that further. She made beautiful crafts around her, I thought at times she didn't have crafted herself alone, I knew that she not only made her life beautiful but also mine which made me be in good nature, well-mannered, and being humble to others, and she made me learn many things. When I cry after letting the pain out, I sprinkle the last teardrops from my eyes with my fingertips, it's not that I do every time but mostly it happens subconsciously yet never felt strange until she imitated me one day in college. After I cried, and sprinkled the last tears to make the normal atmosphere back for myself, she imitated how I cried, and somehow, I felt a bit strange feeling how odd that looks, and we ended up laughing. Now, after I cry, and to gain back myself, I sprinkle the tears, and look for her response as if she were doing the same, and teasing me. I laugh out loud then.

The world became a rented house that I'm unable to pay for. When I hear I love you, and I hate you from her, I feel them as the most valuable words for me because it's her true words where both the words shower only love. Sometimes after fights she used to open up less, and that's when she missed my presence. Now her absence makes me feel her presence too. "My hand always lifts up unknowingly seek yours to take me, and let me walk beside you just like every time." It's weird. Of course, isn't it? But for me this thought makes me gain myself back. Just like an amputee looks at his body part, and recalls memories with it, I recall myself being with her. At times, we feel like the past days were beautiful. It's because we don't get a chance to live in that once again, and our feelings are such type, we want memories that we were in.

# 39

Whenever I laugh hard, I can sense a sort of unhappiness deep inside which tells me continuously that I'm missing her each, and every moment. Even in my crying she's helping me by making my eyes keen, and clear out of dust. Why is she so kind to a girl who couldn't protect her? I never knew that an empty road would last for longer in my life, which once made me think of the future. I used to love the combination of rain, and long road travel, but now I'm scared that I can't see it in such a combination. Whatever I think, the thought runs, and swings towards her, and gets interlinked, pushbacks an outcome of her memories in the end. Soon entering the class, my eyes used to search for her, and so she did. Now, I feel like I saw her yesterday, and if today is Sunday, we will meet again tomorrow. I know this distance is far yet I don't let her go out of my memories. I thought the world would stop but it's not the world which stopped, it's just me. Somewhere I'm also traveling which is filled with her memories.

After a few days, I observed the world being busy in its mechanical life, and there was me who is staring out peculiarly, just a blank thought where I escaped in her thoughts. If she gets to know that I came for her on that day she would have thought, "Why couldn't you take a step earlier just like this day!" To call this as destiny or my own fault I somehow missed my happiness, and have no explanation for the questions. "When I touch some girl in a casual way it makes me remind of you wishing for your presence, and this thought makes me take a bit distance from others, and I can't offer my shoulder to anyone who is low because the place is only reserved for you and that's it, as of now, I can't imagine someone leaning on my shoulder instead of you. Without hurting, I simply lean a bit back not letting the person know what I feel because we never know when a simple word in our view could hurt others so I never try to hurt anyone, and you know you are that person for me for whom I can't cry in front of others. When I see people dressing up like you, I feel like going, and hugging the one but deep inside I know it's not you as those sharp eyes weren't gazing at me. Do you know how it hurts my heart, and gives me an ache? Yes, I do agree you suffered more than me, and I deserve the pain. Still, I face a mini world war everyday not to call out your name while speaking to others because I know I will end up in pain again."

"Everything looks so familiar, the surroundings, casual talks but the only difference is you are not there beside me, you stay within me, and this difference somehow affects me very hard just like a sword in my heart, and it holds in my heart so strong. The Sun rose, flowers started blooming, birds were humming, workers were going to the office as their daily routine nothing seemed changed, only within me everything changed." Thereafter, life took two moods when it rains, I feel fear of remembering that day, and the other thing is somehow she is making a way through rain to touch me, this is when I feel dilemma whether to go into the rain, and accept her as nature or shut inside my room, and not let that rain drops remind me of that day again in my life. In this struggle I accept my mood swings. When I feel like going into the rain I go, and enjoy it, and if not; I deny it, and stick back.

"I'm happy that you gave me the best part in your life, I'm happy to be a part of your memories, I'm happy that you thought of me wholeheartedly just because of that I'm living in a life that I lived with you. I'm happy for each, and every minute we spent. My shoulder awaits your presence to lean on it, and I close my eyes to talk to you. Only you yourself can replace the place in my heart. You are my blood flow, maybe my heart skips a beat but the flow of my blood never stops until I die so I don't want to lose you for a nano second as well. You are like transformation just like energy transforms you too transform from one energy to the other. Until I breathe, I'll be waiting for you, once I stop, I'll be there with you."

"I remember you used to take your hands off mine when you were in a bad mood not to let your pain pass my sense, and to talk about it. The words that you said make me feel numb, you said once in a casual talk, we can realize, and appreciate the living organism only when it disappears from the Earth. God takes the people whom he loves the most. If we are still alive, it means there's some other person in this world who loves us more than him. Maybe you were true, now I cry out of pain, and remember your good nature yet can't tell you anymore for the first thing you said, and my love was not sufficient to make you to be with me. Tears come seldom, at times for certain incidents I feel so numb that tears can't shed, I just accept it, and take things easy. I feel like I became mechanical with low feelings. A woman's heart is as deep as the ocean, the more one tries to dive in, the more he can explore but at some points I might haven't been that deep to your heart, and that results into this day for me. Always battle takes place between my mind, and heart in which heart always wins following emotions, and your memories. When a child without parents is called an orphan then what does a person with a friend only in thoughts be called? I don't want to google it. I just questioned myself for some reasons. When a friend doesn't come to college for a single day with a proper reason, the whole day becomes a hell to the other person who misses him/her. What if the waiting continues for a long life? Grief inside kills like no other slow poison, and the relief comes once the last breath is taken, feels calm aftermath. Every place is being so reserved as if I went to another unknown world where everyone just seems familiar yet can't become closer."

When I think of her, I get a glimpse of her eyes first. She had black eyeballs with honey-colored finishing which only few people can observe when they look into her deep eyes, and a mole at the end of her eyebrow put a beauty spot on her face. Some memories, and some people are not that easily forgettable, and sometimes pain is also happiness.

In my life, she resembles a tittle (the tiny dot in lower case of alphabet letters such as "i") though a small part of my life, her presence makes me complete. For me, I can be perfect with her with my own imperfections, and without her I'm that single that I can't accompany others, even though I accompany I feel as a third wheel.

I used to tell her when she was low, "You have that will power to face the pain, soon you will have multiples of happiness ahead." Today is something different that I told her, I'm even scared to feel her touch as I may miss that feeling. Her inner beauty is that she didn't even let her pain out thinking that it may hurt others, and very few personalities do have this mindset of not hurting others even though they are hurt. In the end, she felt that people will remember her in wrong perception for some reasons but I want my Sona to be remembered with all the good in her. I strongly agree that people may appear a bit strange to others but that's not when we are supposed to judge a person, to say a word about someone we first have to be them, and I believe we won't get an option to judge instead we accept everyone. Deep inside in our imaginations, everyone has a subconscious person who wants to come out, and explore the world but because of our surroundings or some other constraints the person stays within. Once we allow him to come out, wonders happen, just allow all the good within you to burst out.

The mythologies that were written are for the recollection of the past, and bravery of some great personalities, and the book I wrote is in remembrance of her. She appears when I close my eyes, she appears when I open my eyes with tears, she appears in my thoughts, and dreams, and I never miss her because she is *My Only One*.

She said what the society thinks, now I want the whole world to know her inner beauty.

She is as sacred as river
as pure as air
as powerful as fire
as broad as the Sky, and
as tolerant as the Earth.

# 40

Your love, your presence in my life makes me a better person every day. Those memories shine as sparkles with each sparkle holding a bit of your memories. I always remember the first time I saw your beautiful face turning around, and giggling, you walking out of the auditorium, the scene makes me remember the sound of your anklet beads that day, resonates with the sound of my heart that beats till this day. Let me cry until the last eye drop cries for you, and as I never cried so hard, one day I want to cry by leaning my head on your shoulder, and hugging you, sobbing inside is a hell but I want to hold you, and cry so the day I cry the most, be with me, and let's go to the beautiful place where you live now, and we shall restart the life again by adding tremendous memories in the next phase of life.

I believe we are one soul just as you said, to keep that word, let our aftermath also be remembered for our soul connection, and being friends forever. This book shall be the evidence for all the memories we carry in our hearts. I wish one day we can read this together, even if it lasts for ages, I will wait for you. The people out there reading this be blessed with long lives together with their friends. Finally, my girl, this is for you, we shall make abundance of memories just like every time for the rest of our lives.